# When Strong Women Speak, Strong Women Listen

## Inspired Words of Wisdom for Women on Life, Love, Happiness, and Success

### Adriana Fuentes Díaz

Caliente Press

*To My Beautiful Inspiring Daughter! ♥ With hope that there will be many Strong Women around you, who Listen ♥*

*Love Mom*

# When Strong Women Speak, Strong Women Listen

Copyright ©2020 Adriana Fuentes Díaz

ISBN: 978-1-943702-71-8 (Print edition)
      978-1-943702-75-6 (Kindle edition)

All rights reserved. No part of this publication may be reproduced, distributed or transmitted in any form or by any means, including photocopying, recording, or other electronic or mechanical methods, without the prior written permission of the publisher, except in the case of brief quotations embodied in critical reviews and certain other noncommercial uses permitted by copyright law. For permission requests, write to the publisher, addressed "Attention: Permissions Coordinator," at the address below.

Published by:
Caliente Press
1775 E Palm Canyon Drive, Suite 110-198
Palm Springs, CA 92264
U.S.A.
Email: steven@CalientePress.com

Cover Illustration: Berenice Lacroix
Cover Design: Héctor Castañeda

ENDORSEMENTS AND PRAISE

Adriana did a great job in consolidating the best quotes from the best women we have known and heard of. She carefully chose quotes with meaningful words so that they resonate in our minds. Women are the best mentors, coaches, teachers to other women, because we know our challenges, we understand our fears and insecurities. And most important, we know what comfort us.

So for every woman out there, use this book to get that comfort, to overcome your challenges and fears, and to be coached by the strongest women the universe has brought...including you. Thank you Adriana for this powerful book.

**Ileana Ferber**
**Woman, Mother, Wife, Daughter, Friend, Student**
**Professional Specialist in Local Economic Development**
**Advocate for Women Economic Empowerment**
**U.S.A.**

I really liked this compilation of phrases from different authors, especially because they are classified by areas, which makes it very easy to search specifically for a topic related to love, friendships, success, gratitude, values, among others.

I find it a very fresh, and friendly book that helps us to reflect on important concepts and values for the development and empowerment of the female gender. Congrats Adriana great job.

**Julie De Armas**
**Clinical Psychologist and Coach**
**Madrid, Spain**

Adriana self-realized in the same way that she made a commitment to inspire all women with this wonderful book. Proud to have been her first boss in the advertising world.

Adriana, grateful for your friendship. I admire you and I celebrate with you this great achievement.

**Beatriz Resler**
**Advertising Director**
**Israel**

At a time when all of humanity is submerged in total confusion and where many times it seems that the good news and positive thoughts that return us to our pure essence are gone, Adriana shows us that if we listen to ourselves in the echoing of an incredible, powerful, and challenging feminine voice, we can return to our center and reinterpret our history, even leading us to change our own. *When Strong Women Speak, Strong Women Listen* is a compendium of phrases that reflect the great power of communication and human sensitivity that Adriana innately has with her. Thank you Adri for demonstrating through your book the enormous power of words in the soul.

**Francisco Partida**
**Communication Advisor, Strategist & Marketing**
**Mexico**

It's so refreshing to see pages and pages of quotes by dynamic women. Too often women's voices are silenced. When *Strong Women Speak, Strong Women Listen* provides you with encouragement to overcome life's challenges. Refer to the motivational quotes daily for inspiration.

**Lynn Schmidt, PhD**
**Award-winning author of *Thriving from A to Z:***
***Best Practices to Increase Resilience, Satisfaction, and***
***Success***
**U.S.A.**

Adriana's thoughtful, beautiful book takes on our deepest concerns as women with wisdom and measured perspective. I love her set-up of each section and the hand-picked quotations are easily dipped-into at times of need and provide inspiration and grounding.

You will never feel alone in the world with this book at your bedside.

**Anne Sandberg**
**Managing Director**
**Predict Success**
**U.S.A.**

The natural essence of women is mystical, co-creative, we constantly reinvent ourselves and always, when a woman who inspires us speaks, we all remain silent.

Thanks to the magic of the word, women dance in a dance of harmony and freedom. This book is intended to transform the spirit of those who read it.

**Ann Muller**
**Founder and CEO**
**Air Femme Magazine**
**Mexico**

# Contents

| | |
|---|---|
| Introduction | 13 |
| My Story | 17 |
| Love | 19 |
| Love Quotes | 21 |
| Friendship | 35 |
| Friendship Quotes | 37 |
| Inspirational | 47 |
| Inspirational Quotes | 49 |
| Happiness | 65 |
| Happiness Quotes | 67 |
| Life | 77 |
| Life Quotes | 79 |
| Success | 93 |
| Success Quotes | 95 |
| Gratitude | 109 |
| Gratitude Quotes | 111 |
| Truth | 123 |
| Truth Quotes | 125 |
| Values | 137 |
| Values Quotes | 139 |
| Forgiveness | 151 |
| Forgiveness Quotes | 153 |
| Adriana's Favorite Sayings | 163 |
| Acknowledgements | 167 |
| About the Author | 169 |

# *Dedication*

This book was created to inspire all women, especially those who fight to better themselves, those who suffer, those who laugh, those who cry, and those who fall and rise many times.

This book is a gift for the best woman in the world, my Mother, the one who always guides me, advises me, corrects me, gives me her shoulder to cry and laugh too.

The one who educated me and gave me everything and much more than what she had. Thanks to her, I am here to inspire all of you to be happy, successful, and to never give up.

*Feet, what do I need you for when I have wings to fly?*

Frida Kahlo

# Introduction

I opened this book with one of my favorite Frida Kahlo quotes, for she has inspired me throughout my life. Her quote has continuously reminded me that I can fly over any hurdle, obstacle, difficulty, or challenge that life throws at me.

At different stages of my life, many women of different nationalities, professions, ages, cultures, races, and education have given me the necessary motivation, courage, and strength to keep going through their wise words and strong examples.

As I think back over recent history, I realize the difficult roles and challenges that women have had, both personally and professionally, to help us women gain our rightful place in society. I admire and value these strong women and what our gender has achieved. From being able to vote, to how to decide for our own professional and personal futures are great steps in which we should all feel proud.

Because of the progressive actions of women in developed countries to access formal education, we have gained a fundamental platform that provided them with a very powerful weapon of training and information, through which we have channeled our aspirations, desires for social improvement, and political demands. There is no doubt that education, training, and access to information has also helped women integrate and, to an extent, advance in many labor markets as well.

However, despite the advances we have made in the more developed countries of the world, there is still much to do and work to leave to the new generations of girls a world with greater equity and inclusion, less gender violence, and greater participation and leadership in all aspects of society.

Surely it will not be an easy task either, but when we sow the best fruits, we will obtain the best harvests. All generations of young women must be supported, motivated, and encouraged to pursue their dreams and goals; since there is nothing impossible in life that cannot be achieved with discipline, perseverance, and inspiration.

I also believe that it is time for women to proactively help and support other women more. We need to be more solidary, united, and encouraging as a gender. We need to stop being competitive with one another. And, above all, we need to learn to respect ourselves as women and human beings.

I am who I am today, because each person who has entered my life has touched it in a different and special way. I am grateful for the wonderful people I have had at my side in this journey that is life. The blows, learning, and experiences are part of it and make us learn to be more humble, honest, loving, and better human beings.

In this book I will write about the values that give life meaning. Human values are what demonstrate the kind of person we are. Some of these values are gratitude, truth, love, friendship, and others that I consider very important.

The world in which we live today unfortunately suffers more and more every day from a lack of these values, as too many people seem to place greater importance on selfishness, personal interests, and indifference towards others.

While I believe all the sources for the quotations in this book to be reliable, readers should not interpret *When Strong Women Speak, Strong Women Listen* to be a highly researched, authoritative reference book. This is not what I set out to do and it is certainly not what I have delivered.

What I have set out to do is gather and share the quotes that moved me, impressed me, or got me thinking a bit harder, deeper, or even more lightly. In achieving this endeavor, I trust you will agree, *When Strong Women Speak, Strong Women Listen* does deliver.

For my personal and professional goals, I have always sought to stay inspired to achieve each of my projects. I now want to inspire, with this book and my future endeavors, many more women around the world.

Finally, I hope I have made this book an excellent gift for your mother, daughter, best friend, sister, cousin, or colleague. My idea is that *When Strong Women Speak, Strong Women Listen* will serve as inspiration for many women in your life and for the next generations of women who will surely have an increasingly important and leading role in this world.

Adriana Fuentes Díaz
August 2020

# My Story

I was born in Mexico City, but I grew up in Venezuela, a place in which I was happy for 35 years. Its climate, people, and the beauty of its land gave me the best years of my life. I also lived in Newark, Delaware, and Montreal.

I had the opportunity to work in two excellent multinational companies, HBO (Sony Entertainment TV) and BBDO. In both, I learned, traveled, and grew a lot as a professional. I was surrounded by incredible people, who were very capable, professional, and humane.

After the very fast, sad, and depressing deterioration in Venezuela, I decided to start a new life. I left Caracas at the age of 38 with four suitcases, my son, and my beautiful dog Cala to return to Mexico City. I journeyed into an unknown adventure, where I carried with me only my good attitude, faith, and a belief in myself and my potential as both a woman and a professional, combined with the desire for success as my main tools. Some members of my family did not agree with that decision, but the most important thing at the time was I believed in myself.

A few years later, as I look back and remember that moment as if it had been yesterday, I realize how strong and determined women can be when we pursue our dreams. Sometimes, we do not value ourselves in the face of many difficult circumstances that happen in our lives. But, it is in these situations, that we need a little more belief and appreciation for "our-self."

Now, with 15 years of experience in several companies in the corporate world, in both national and regional positions, I am reinventing myself and focusing on what I am really passionate about. This includes writing, traveling, helping the most helpless people and animals, and the field of decoration and details. I now realize life is too short to waste on dedicating ourselves to anything that does not make us happy.

A few months ago I launched my decoration blog (www.decoracionyalgomas.com) where week after week I give ideas and tips on how to decorate the different spaces of your house, office, or garden with a low budget and original and different details.

Finally, I feel very fortunate in each and every one of the personal and professional experiences I have had in my life. Thanks to each one of them, I have learned to be braver, stronger, persistent, optimistic, happy, and to fight tirelessly for my dreams.

I hope you enjoy this book as much as I do and, above all, it inspires you in everything you do and set out in life. My very best wishes to you.

CHAPTER 1

# Love

I consider love to be one of the most important values among living beings. It is the force that drives us to do things well, that is why it is considered a value that has a very clear difference between good and evil.

Love is a moral feeling, because it induces us to try to act well in our life and with the people we love. In addition, it leads us to have a life full of peace, tranquility, joy and, consequently, well-being with ourselves and with others.

In the same way it is a feeling of universal affection that one has towards a person, animal, or thing.

Love also refers to a feeling of emotional and sexual attraction that you have towards a person with whom you want to have a relationship or coexistence.

Unconditional love happens when a person makes a total commitment to another without expecting anything in return. An example of unconditional love for a religious person is their love for God. Another is the love of a father or a mother towards a child. These are forms of love that are considered unique and special.

Self-love is spoken of in reference to acceptance, respect, perceptions, courage, positive thoughts, and self-esteem. It is a feeling that we must be able to recognize and that those around us must be able to appreciate.

Unfortunately as a society, we have not fully understood the depth and the true meaning of this great word. For, if we did we would take more care of our planet, our environment, we would help our communities more, we would think more about our societies, and we would be less selfish people.

If we lived with greater love for one another, we would contribute to live in a world with fewer wars, more peace, love, respect, and understanding with all living things on the planet. Love is in everything that surrounds us and if we learned to perceive that love a little more, we would be happier women and men. And the world would become a better place for future generations to inherit.

---

*You have to learn to love yourself before you can love someone else. Because it's only when we love ourselves that we feel worthy of someone else's love.*

Alyssa B. Sheinmel

# Love Quotes

We need to learn how to love one another and accept one another.
**Ellen DeGeneres**

What I cannot love, I overlook.
**Anaïs Nin**

I saw that you were perfect, and so I love you. Then I saw that you were not perfect and I loved you even more.
**Angelita Lim**

A successful marriage is not a gift; it is an achievement.
**Ann Landers**

In loving one another through our works we bring an increase of grace and growth in divine love
**Mother Teresa**

The best and most beautiful things in this world cannot be seen or even heard, but must be felt with the heart.
**Helen Keller**

One act of beneficence, one act of real usefulness, is worth all the abstract sentiment in the world.
**Ann Radcliffe**

I love the silent hour of night, for blissful dreams may then arise, revealing to my charmed sight what may not bless my waking eyes.
**Anne Brontë**

You deserve a lover who wants you disheveled, with everything and all the reasons that wake you up in a haste and the demons that won't let you sleep.
**Frida Kahlo**

Love is the great miracle cure. Loving ourselves works miracles in our lives.
**Louise L. Hay**

Love and kindness are never wasted. They always make a difference.
**Barbara De Angelis**

I never think of myself as an icon. What is in other people's minds is not in my mind. I just do my thing.
**Audrey Hepburn**

Everyone has inside of him a piece of good news. The good news is that you don't know how great you can be! How much you can love! What you can accomplish! And what your potential is!
**Anne Frank**

Man is an end in himself. Romantic love — the profound, exalted, lifelong passion that unites his mind and body in the sexual act — is the living testimony to that principle.
**Ayn Rand**

Talk to yourself like you would to someone you love.
**Brené Brown**

A successful marriage requires falling in love many times, always with the same person.
**Mignon McLaughlin**

Love is the expression of one's values, the greatest reward you can earn for the moral qualities you have achieved in your character and person, the emotional price paid by one man for the joy he receives from the virtues of another.
**Ayn Rand**

You never lose by loving. You always lose by holding back.
**Barbara De Angelis**

I may not always be offered work, but I'll always have my family.
**Audrey Hepburn**

The most important part of the body is the brain. Of my face, I like the eyebrows and eyes.
**Frida Kahlo**

After the verb *to Love*, *to Help* is the most beautiful verb in the world.
**Bertha von Suttner**

You are imperfect, you are wired for struggle, but you are worthy of love and belonging.
**Brené Brown**

If only you knew how beautiful you are unconditionally. Don't you know it's enough if all you do is breathe?
**Brittany Burgunder**

The whole point of marriage is to encourage your partner's development and have them encourage yours.
**Carol Dweck**

Above all challenge yourself. You may well surprise yourself at what strengths you have, what you can accomplish.
**Cecile Springer**

I don't need anyone else to distract me from myself anymore, like I always thought I would.
**Charlotte Eriksson**

The problem lies not in the question, "What is the meaning of life?" The problem is not finding Love as the answer.
**Debbie Skelly**

What is a hero without love for mankind.
**Doris Lessing**

Beauty is only skin deep, but ugly goes clean to the bone.
**Dorothy Parker**

If you have love in your life, it can make up for a great many things you lack. If you don't have it, no matter what else there is, it is not enough.
**Ann Landers**

He who angers you conquers you.
**Elizabeth Kenny**

Embrace who you are. Literally. Hug yourself. Accept who you are.
**Ellen DeGeneres**

I have never met a person whose greatest need was anything other than real, unconditional love. You can find it in a simple act of kindness toward someone who needs help. There is no mistaking love. You feel it in your heart. It is the common fiber of life, the flame that heals our soul, energizes our spirit and supplies passion to our lives.
**Elisabeth Kübler-Ross**

Age does not protect you from love. But love, to some extent, protects you from age.
**Anaïs Nin**

Staying vulnerable is a risk we have to take if we want to experience connection.
**Brené Brown**

True love is not a strong, fiery, impetuous passion. It is, on the contrary, an element calm and deep…it is wise and discriminating, and its devotion is real and abiding.
**Ellen G. White**

You are not born with beauty, your beauty is created by who you are. Your inner beauty is more important than how people see you on the outside.
**Emily Coussons**

If you aren't good at loving yourself, you will have a difficult time loving anyone, since you'll resent the time and energy you give another person that you aren't even giving to yourself.
**Barbara De Angelis**

Take a lover who looks at you like maybe you are a bourbon biscuit.
**Frida Kahlo**

It's not how much we give but how much love we put into giving.
**Mother Teresa**

You deserve a lover who makes you feel safe, who can consume this world whole if he walks hand in hand with you; someone who believes that his embraces are a perfect match with your skin.
**Frida Kahlo**

If they hadn't told me I was ugly, I never would have searched for my beauty. And if they hadn't tried to break me down, I wouldn't know that I'm unbreakable.
**Gabourey Sidibe**

Beauty is the shadow of God on the universe.
**Gabriela Mistral**

There is no democracy in any love relation: only mercy.
**Gillian Rose**

Cooking is like love. It should be entered into with abandon or not at all.
**Harriet Van Horne**

We could never learn to be brave and patient, if there were only joy in the world.
**Helen Keller**

Sometimes I wonder what my life would be like without you. Then I thank God I only have to wonder.
**Heather Cordelia**

A kiss is a lovely trick designed by nature to stop speech when words become superfluous.
**Ingrid Bergman**

True love doesn't come to you it has to be inside you.
**Julia Roberts**

It's what you choose to believe that makes you the person you are.
**Karen Marie Moning**

What can you do to promote world peace? Go home and love your family.
**Mother Teresa**

Love is a battle with yourself. Be kind and love yourself before you love anyone else.
**Karen Quan**

When you connect with that love and that compassion, that's when everything unfolds.
**Ellen DeGeneres**

Love only yourself a little bit longer, until you can't stand not to love someone else.
**Kiera Cass**

If you obey all the rules, you miss all the fun.
**Katharine Hepburn**

Hope is love's happiness, but not its life.
**Letitia E. Landon**

Love thy neighbor as thyself, but choose your neighborhood.
**Louise Beal**

Breathe. Let go. And remind yourself that this very moment is the only one you know you have for sure.
**Oprah Winfrey**

To say "I love you" one must know first how to say the "I."
**Ayn Rand**

Be faithful in small things because it is in them that your strength lies.
**Mother Teresa**

Love is a force more formidable than any other. It is invisible – it cannot be seen or measured, yet it is powerful enough to transform you in a moment, and offer you more joy than any material possession could.
**Barbara De Angelis**

I love myself for I am a beloved child of the universe and the universe lovingly takes care of me now.
**Louise L. Hay**

If you don't love yourself, you'll always be chasing after people who don't love you either.
**Mandy Hale**

If it is your time, love will track you down like a cruise missile.
**Lynda Barry**

Loving yourself...does not mean being self-absorbed or narcissistic, or disregarding others. Rather it means welcoming yourself as the most honored guest in your own heart, a guest worthy of respect, a lovable companion.
**Margo Anand**

Some think love can be measured by the amount of butterflies in their tummy. Others think love can be measured in bunches of flowers, or by using the words "for ever." But love can only truly be measured by actions. It can be a small thing, such as peeling an orange for a person you love because you know they don't like doing it.
**Marian Keyes**

Every day use your magic to be of service to others.
**Marcia Wieder**

Love is what we are born with. Fear is what we learn. The spiritual journey is the unlearning of fear and prejudices and the acceptance of love back in our hearts. Love is the essential reality and our purpose on earth. To be consciously aware of it, to experience love in ourselves and others, is the meaning of life. Meaning does not lie in things. Meaning lies in us.
**Marianne Williamson**

Each of us must work for his own improvement, and at the same time share a general responsibility for all humanity.
**Marie Curie**

You can take no credit for beauty at sixteen. But if you are beautiful at sixty, it will be your soul's own doing.
**Marie Stopes**

A commitment to love and justice demands the transformation of social structures as well as of hearts.
**Mary E. Hunt**

To be kind to all, to like many and love a few, to be needed and wanted by those we love, is certainly the nearest we can come to happiness.
**Mary Stuart**

Before you were conceived I wanted you. Before you were born I loved you. Before you were here for an hour I would die for you. This is the miracle of life.
**Maureen Hawkins**

Love opens the doors into everything including, and perhaps most of all, the door into one's own secret, and often terrible and frightening, real self.
**May Sarton**

If we pray, we will believe; If we believe, we will love; If we love, we will serve.
**Mother Teresa**

Don't settle for a relationship that won't let you be yourself.
**Oprah Winfrey**

Love is never supposed to hurt. Love is supposed to heal, to be your haven from misery, to make living fucking worthwhile.
**Mia Asher**

The beauty of a woman is not in a facial mode but the true beauty in a woman is reflected in her soul. It is the caring that she lovingly gives the passion that she shows. The beauty of a woman grows with the passing years.
**Audrey Hepburn**

When you are your own best friend, you don't endlessly seek out relationships, friendships, and validation from the wrong sources because you realize that the only approval and validation you need is your own.
**Mandy Hale**

To love is to value. Only a rationally selfish man, a man of self-esteem, is capable of love — because he is the only man capable of holding firm, consistent, uncompromising, unbetrayed values. The man who does not value himself, cannot value anything or anyone.
**Ayn Rand**

You can only become truly accomplished at something you love. Don't make money your goal. Instead, pursue the things you love doing and then do them so well that people can't take their eyes off of you.
**Maya Angelou**

The hardest learned lesson: that people have only their kind of love to give, not our kind.
**Mignon McLaughlin**

Spread the love of God through your life but only use words when necessary.
**Mother Teresa**

Spend time understanding who you are, after all the only person you're ever going to truly live with; is yourself.
**Nikki Rowe**

Love and kindness are never wasted. They always make a difference. They bless the one who receives them, and they bless you, the giver.
**Barbara De Angelis**

When a poor person dies of hunger it has not happened because God did not take care of him or her. It has happened because neither you nor I wanted to give that person what he or she needed.
**Mother Teresa**

True love is usually the most inconvenient kind.
**Kiera Cass**

Love yourself enough to have a meaningful life.
**Millen Livis**

Loneliness is the leprosy of the modern world.
**Mother Teresa**

If he can't handle you at your worst then he does not deserve you at your best. Real love means seeing beyond the words spoken out of pain, and instead seeing a person's soul.
**Shannon L. Alder**

Some souls just understand each other upon meeting.
**N. R. Hart**

When you realize you want to spend the rest of your life with somebody, you want the rest of your life to start as soon as possible.
**Nora Ephron**

Honesty and transparency make you vulnerable. Be honest and transparent anyway.
**Mother Teresa**

I've come to believe that each of us has a personal calling that's as unique as a fingerprint — and that the best way to succeed is to discover what you love and then find a way to offer it to others in the form of service, working hard, and also allowing the energy of the universe to lead you.
**Oprah Winfrey**

The fruit of Silence is Prayer; the fruit of Prayer is Faith; the fruit of Faith is Love; the fruit of Love is Service; the fruit of Service is Peace.
**Mother Teresa**

I had to grow to love my body. I did not have a good self-image at first. Finally it occurred to me, I'm either going to love me or hate me. And I chose to love myself. Then everything kind of sprung from there. Things that I thought weren't attractive became sexy. Confidence makes you sexy.
**Queen Latifah**

Maybe if we love ourselves healthy we will all heal?
**Nikki Rowe**

To accept ourselves as we are means to value our imperfections as much as our perfections.
**Sandra Bierig**

You are not an option, a choice or a soft place to land after a long battle. You were meant to be the one. If you can wrap yourself around the idea that you are something incredible, then you will stop excusing behavior that rapes your very soul. You were never meant to teach someone to love you. You were meant to be loved.
**Shannon L. Alder**

I have found the paradox, that if you love until it hurts, there can be no more hurt, only more love.
**Mother Teresa**

Love's a choice. Make wise decisions.
**Shellie R. Warren**

You can never meet your potential until you truly learn to love yourself.
**Teresa Collins**

Love makes your soul crawl out from its hiding place.
**Zora Neale Hurston**

If we want a love message to be heard, it has got to be sent out. To keep a lamp burning, we have to keep putting oil in it.
**Mother Teresa**

Plant your own garden and decorate your own soul, instead of waiting for someone to bring you flowers.
**Veronica A. Shoffstall**

No need to hurry. No need to sparkle. No need to be anybody but yourself.
**Virginia Woolf**

Nobody has ever measured, not even poets, how much the heart can hold.
**Zelda Fitzgerald**

Self-love is complete forgiveness, acceptance and respect for who you are deep down — all your beautiful and hideous parts included.
**Aletheia Luna**

If you judge people, you have no time to love them.
**Mother Teresa**

I love you more than my own skin.
**Frida Kahlo**

CHAPTER 2

# Friendship

Friendship is an emotional relationship that can be established between two or more people, to which fundamental values such as love, loyalty, solidarity, unconditionally, sincerity, and commitment are associated. It is cultivated with treatment and reciprocal interest over time.

Friendship can arise between men and women, boyfriends, husbands, relatives with any kind of bond, people of different ages, religions, ideologies, cultures, socio-economic level etc. Even, a friendship can be established between a human being and an animal (not for nothing the dog is man's best friend!).

Friendships, however, have different degrees of rapport. From the friends with whom we have more distant relationships, to those with whom the treatment is so close that we consider them "best friends," giving that friendship a degree of superiority and meaningfulness over other friends.

Friendship not only arises with those who have more affinities in terms of tastes and interests, or with whom we have more similarity, but can appear between very different people.

In fact, sometimes that is a factor that strengthens friendship, because a good friendship complements and enriches the person, not only in the exchange of ideas, information and feelings, but also in the fact of sharing the good and bad moments in the course of life.

True friendship has become a utopian theme in this globalized world of relationships based on immediacy and superficiality, where we are increasingly unable to put aside our interests and truly build a lasting and solid bond of friendship.

When there is a true friendship, friends recognize each other as "great friends." Great friends are those whose level of loyalty, attention, care, and affection is higher than normal. It is the one that is counted on for life and is present at all times.

Love and friendship have much in common, including deep affection, respect, loyalty, and a sense of commitment. In fact, in friendship there is always love and in love, there is usually friendship.

Really, friendship is a great treasure that we can all possess and therefore we must appreciate, value, and above all, know how to preserve these relationships over time.

Definitely a good friendship is a gift of life.

---

*My friends have made the story of my life.*
*In a thousand ways they have turned my limitations*
*into beautiful privileges.*

Helen Keller

When Strong Women Speak. Strong Women Listen.

# Friendship Quotes

No person is your friend who demands your silence, or denies your right to grow.
**Alice Walker**

Find a group of people who challenge and inspire you; spend a lot of time with them, and it will change your life.
**Amy Poehler**

Each friend represents a world in us, a world possibly not born until they arrive.
**Anaïs Nin**

Don't listen to people — feel them. Lips may lie, hearts tell the truth.
**Anita Krizzan**

Some people arrive and make such a beautiful impact on your life, you can barely remember what life was like without them.
**Anna Taylor**

Call it a clan, call it a network, call it a tribe, call it a family. Whatever you call it, whoever you are, you need one.
**Jane Howard**

Be kind to unkind people — they need it the most.
**Ashleigh Brilliant**

You will discover that you have two hands. One is for helping yourself and the other is for helping others.
**Audrey Hepburn**

A friend is somebody you want to be around when you feel like being by yourself.
**Barbara Burrow**

To handle yourself, use your head; to handle others, use your heart.
**Eleanor Roosevelt**

Sometimes, with luck, we find the kind of true friend, male or female, that appears only two or three times in a lucky lifetime, one that will winter us and summer us, grieve, rejoice, and travel with us.
**Barbara Holland**

Never explain yourself. Your friends don't need it and your enemies won't believe it.
**Belgicia Howell**

Connection is why we're here. It's what gives purpose and meaning to our lives.
**Brené Brown**

You're always with yourself, so you might as well enjoy the company.
**Diane von Furstenberg**

A friend is someone who knows the song in your heart and can sing it back to you when you have forgotten the words.
**Donna Roberts**

Love is like quicksilver in the hand. Leave the fingers open and it stays. Clutch it, and it darts away.
**Dorothy Parker**

One's life has value so long as one attributes value to the life of others, by means of love, friendship, and compassion.
**Simone de Beauvoir**

The giving of love is an education in itself.
**Eleanor Roosevelt**

Let us always meet each other with smile, for the smile is the beginning of love.
**Mother Teresa**

Nobody sees a flower — really — it is so small it takes time — we haven't time — and to see takes time, like to have a friend takes time.
**Georgia O'Keeffe**

All love that has not friendship for its base, is like a mansion built upon the sand.
**Ella Wheeler Wilcox**

Give me one friend, just one, who meets the needs of all my varying moods.
**Esther M. Clark**

The best time to make friends is before you need them.
**Ethel Barrymore**

Friendship is a strong and habitual inclination in two persons to promote the good and happiness of one another.
**Eustace Budgell**

A friend can tell you things you don't want to tell yourself.
**Frances Ward Weller**

Women understand. We may share experiences, make jokes, paint pictures, and describe humiliations that mean nothing to men, but women understand. The odd thing about these deep and personal connections of women is that they often ignore barriers of age, economics, worldly experience, race, culture — all the barriers that, in male or mixed society, had seemed so difficult to cross.
**Gloria Steinem**

A friend is someone who makes it easy to believe in yourself.
**Heidi Wills**

Walking with a friend in the dark is better than walking alone in the light.
**Helen Keller**

The real test of friendship is: Can you literally do nothing with the other person? Can you enjoy together those moments of life that are utterly simple? They are the moments people look back on at the end of life and number as their most sacred experiences.
**Eugene Kennedy**

In my friend, I find a second self.
**Isabel Norton**

It takes a great deal of bravery to stand up to our enemies, but just as much to stand up to our friends.
**J. K. Rowling**

There is nothing I wouldn't do for those who are really my friends. I have no notion of loving people by halves; it is not my nature.
**Jane Austen**

Friendship between women is different than friendship between men. It's my women friends that keep starch in my spine and without them, I don't know where I would be.
**Jane Fonda**

This is what I miss, Cordelia: not something that's gone, but something that will never happen. Two old women giggling over their tea.
**Margaret Atwood**

In my day, we didn't have self-esteem, we had self-respect, and no more of it than we had earned.
**Jane Haddam**

The best proof of love is trust.
**Joyce Brothers**

Small gestures can have a big impact. If you walk down the street and smile at someone, that will get passed on to the next person. That has the power to change someone's day.
**Julianna Margulies**

You know it's love when all you want is that person to be happy, even if you're not part of their happiness.
**Julia Roberts**

If you want to find out who's a true friend, screw up or go through a challenging time…then see who sticks around.
**Karen Salmonsohn**

I'm so thankful for friendship. It beautifies life so much.
**L. M. Montgomery**

I think about my best friendship as like a great romance of my young life.
**Lena Dunham**

To be rich in friends is to be poor in nothing.
**Lilian Whiting**

I would rather walk with a friend in the dark, than alone in the light.
**Helen Keller**

The head thinks, the hands labor, but it's the heart that laughs.
**Liz Curtis Higgs**

Female friendships that work are relationships in which women help each other belong to themselves.
**Louise Bernikow**

The women were new friends but I loved them in a massive way. The love was like a large trove of devotion that could only be amassed over time, but it had arrived all at once. The way I loved them felt like it was from long ago.
**Jenny Slate**

True wealth cannot be found in your bank account. It can only be found in those you call friend. Those with whom you share your deepest feelings. And those who accept you for who you really are.
**Mary Vandergrift**

Laugh as much as possible; always laugh. It's the sweetest thing one can do for oneself and one's fellow human beings.
**Maya Angelou**

Don't expect your friend to be a perfect person. But, help your friend to become a perfect person that's true friendship.
**Mother Teresa**

There is nothing better than a friend, unless it is a friend with chocolate.
**Linda Grayson**

Fear makes strangers of those who would be friends.
**Shirley MacLaine**

When a woman becomes her own best friend, life is easier.
**Diane von Furstenberg**

Constant use had not worn ragged the fabric of their friendship.
**Dorothy Parker**

Every time you smile at someone, it is an act of love, a gift to that person, a beautiful thing.
**Mother Teresa**

Friends are a weird thing. It seems like they know all about you, but then they don't understand you at all.
**Natsuo Kirino**

There's something about childhood friends that you just can't replace.
**Lisa Whelchel**

True friends are like diamonds — bright, beautiful, valuable, and always in style.
**Nicole Richie**

Lots of people want to ride with you in the limo — what you want is someone who will take the bus with you when the limo breaks down.
**Oprah Winfrey**

Compromise: The art of dividing a cake in such a way that everybody believes they got the biggest piece.
**Sherry Rothfield**

I believe in angels, the kind that heaven sends. I'm surrounded by angels, and I call them my best friends.
**Pamela Daranjo**

The companions of our childhood always possess a certain power over our minds which hardly any later friend can obtain.
**Mary Wollstonecraft Shelley**

The great thing about new friends is that they bring new energy to your soul.
**Shanna Rodriguez**

Female friendship has been the bedrock of women's lives for as long as there have been women.
**Rebecca Traister**

Do what you can to show you care about other people, and you will make our world a better place.
**Rosalynn Carter**

Abandon the cultural myth that all female friendships must be bitchy, toxic, or competitive. This myth is like heels and purses — pretty but designed to SLOW women down.
**Roxane Gay**

You can love more than one person, she said. That's arguable. Why is it any different from having more than one friend? You're friends with me and you also have other friends, does that mean you don't really value me? I don't have other friends, I said.
**Sally Rooney**

A friendship can weather most things and thrive in thin soil but it needs a little mulch of letters and phone calls and small silly presents every so often to save it from drying out completely.
**Pam Brown**

We are afraid to care too much, for fear that the other person does not care at all.
**Eleanor Roosevelt**

Women instinctively know how to nourish each other, and just being with each other is restorative.
**Tanja Taaljard**

I believe the greatest gift I can conceive of having from anyone is to be seen, heard, understood, and touched by them. The greatest gift I can give is to see, hear, understand, and touch another person.
**Virginia Satir**

I leave you my portrait so that you will have my presence all the days and nights that I am away from you.
**Frida Kahlo**

*Adriana Fuentes Díaz*

CHAPTER 3

# Inspirational

Inspiration is valued in a special way in any creative process in which a spark arises, that is, ideas spring up in a spontaneous and natural way. Any writer or artist makes the most of her moments of inspiration, those moments of work that are totally unpredictable, that is, they do not arise from prior planning.

A writer can take ideas to be inspired by her daily work from everyday situations, through a movie, through a good book, in a conversation with friends ... Inspiration shows that the human being needs to come out of herself to keep constantly learning from others. Interestingly, inspiration often arises after we have given our brains a chance to rest and reset. This is because our minds are not machines designed to generated ideas 24-hours a day.

An inspiration is that which evokes something special in you. A hook that connects to a great idea. Inspiration is nice, yet any artist discovers that there are very few moments of inspiration compared to long hours of work in front of a blank page. Therefore, the best philosophy that any artist has is: "May inspiration find you working." That is to say, to become inspired it is recommended to have a good predisposition to work in relation to regular hour habits, a cozy work environment, and a specific professional routine.

Among the scenarios that are ideal as an inspiration point, it should be noted that nature is a perfect framework of well-being that produces very pleasant sensations and emotions. Being in contact with nature, the mind feels overwhelmed by the perfection of so much beauty. Also, by breathing fresh air, you will feel more relaxed and calm. Connect more with yourself. And in this environment of absolute well-being, ideas will flow better. To have a good inspiration it is essential to be well rested and relaxed.

Being inspired to achieve a successful project, a good grade in school, a freshly baked cake, or the success of anything that you firmly desire, will always be reflected in the passion and inspiration you dedicate to it.

---

*The future belongs to those who believe in the beauty of their dreams.*

Eleanor Roosevelt

# Inspirational Quotes

When we discover that someone we trusted can be trusted no longer, it forces us to reexamine the universe, to question the whole instinct and concept of trust.
**Adrienne Rich**

Vulnerability is the birthplace of innovation, creativity and change.
**Brené Brown**

Belief in oneself is incredibly infectious. It generates momentum, the collective force of which far outweighs any kernel of self-doubt that may creep in.
**Aimee Mullins**

If the motivation is gone, then I am finished.
**Marit Bjørgen**

I want to walk through life instead of being dragged through it.
**Alanis Morissette**

I believe we're all put on this planet for a purpose, and we all have a different purpose.
**Ellen DeGeneres**

Turn your wounds into wisdom.
**Oprah Winfrey**

There's an important difference between giving up and letting go.
**Jessica Hatchigan**

Kindness is always fashionable.
**Amelia Barr**

Anything I cannot transform into something marvelous, I let go.
**Anaïs Nin**

He who loses money, loses much;
He who loses a friend, loses more;
He who loses faith, loses all.
**Eleanor Roosevelt**

If we had no winter, the spring would not be so pleasant; if we did not sometimes taste of adversity, prosperity would not be so welcome.
**Anne Bradstreet**

I know what I want, I have a goal, an opinion, I have a religion and love. Let me be myself and then I am satisfied. I know that I'm a woman, a woman with inward strength and plenty of courage.
**Anne Frank**

Nothing is absolute. Everything changes, everything moves, everything revolves, everything flies and goes away.
**Frida Kahlo**

Although the world is full of suffering, it is full also of the overcoming of it.
**Helen Keller**

I've said it before, but it's absolutely true: my mother gave me my drive, but my father gave me my dreams. Thanks to him, I could see a future.
**Liza Minnelli**

What other people label or might try to call failure, I have learned is just God's way of pointing you in a new direction.
**Oprah Winfrey**

Don't ever wait around for someone else to tell you how to develop yourself.
**April Arnzen**

Music does a lot of things for a lot of people. It's transporting, for sure. It can take you right back, years back, to the very moment certain things happened in your life. It's uplifting, it's encouraging, it's strengthening.
**Aretha Franklin**

Life is full of beauty. Notice it. Notice the bumble bee, the small child, and the smiling faces. Smell the rain, and feel the wind. Live your life to the fullest potential, and fight for your dreams.
**Ashley Smith**

For attractive lips, speak words of kindness.
For lovely eyes, seek out the good in people.
For a slim figure, share your food with the hungry.
For beautiful hair, let a child run their fingers through it.
For poise, walk with the knowledge that you'll never walk alone.
**Audrey Hepburn**

The most depraved type of human being (is) the man without a purpose.
**Ayn Rand**

No matter what age you are, or what your circumstances might be, you are special, and you still have something unique to offer. Your life, because of who you are, has meaning.
**Barbara De Angelis**

Don't be afraid of the space between your dreams and reality. If you can dream it, you can make it so.
**Belva Davis**

I'm not happy, I'm cheerful. There's a difference. A happy woman has no cares at all. A cheerful woman has cares but has learned how to deal with them.
**Beverly Sills**

If you have a talent, use it in every way possible. Don't hoard it. Don't dole it out like a miser. Spend it lavishly, like a millionaire intent on going broke.
**Brenda Francis**

What makes you vulnerable makes you beautiful.
**Brené Brown**

More important than talent, strength or knowledge is the ability to laugh at yourself and enjoy the pursuit of your dreams.
**Amy Grant**

They thought I was a Surrealist, but I wasn't. I never painted dreams. I painted my own reality.
**Frida Kahlo**

Where the myth fails, human love begins. Then we love a human being, not our dream, but a human being with flaws.
**Anaïs Nin**

Faith is a place of mystery, where we find the courage to believe in what we cannot see and the strength to let go of our fear of uncertainty.
**Brené Brown**

Nobody can go back and start a new beginning, but anyone can start today and make a new ending.
**Maria Robinson**

Last night I lost the world, and gained the universe.
**C. JoyBell C.**

Effort is one of those things that gives meaning to life. Effort means you care about something, that something is important to you and you are willing to work for it.
**Carol Dweck**

I hope I will be able to confide everything to you, as I have never been able to confide in anyone, and I hope you will be a great source of comfort and support.
**Anne Frank**

You don't always need a plan. Sometimes you just need to breathe, trust, let go and see what happens.
**Mandy Hale**

I tried always to do better. Saw always a little further. I tried to stretch myself.
**Audrey Hepburn**

The soul always knows how to heal itself. The challenge is to silence the mind.
**Caroline Myss**

I want to believe that there is a mountain so high that I will spend my entire life striving to reach the top of it.
**Cicely Tyson**

If you were born without wings, do nothing to prevent them from growing.
**Coco Chanel**

Holding on is believing that there's only a past; letting go is knowing that there's a future.
**Daphne Rose Kingma**

Healing requires for us to stop struggling, but to enjoy life more and endure it less.
**Darina Stoyanova**

In my books and in romance as a genre, there is a positive, uplifting feeling that leaves the reader with a sense of encouragement and hope for a brighter future — or a brighter present.
**Debbie Macomber**

It's the curiosity that drives me. It's making a difference in the world that prevents me from ever giving up.
**Deborah Meier**

You know there are moments such as these when time stands still and all you do is hold your breath and hope it will wait for you.
**Dorothea Lange**

There are two ways of spreading light: to be the candle or the mirror that reflects it.
**Edith Wharton**

You wouldn't worry so much about what others think of you if your realized how seldom they do.
**Eleanor Roosevelt**

Just don't give up trying to do what you really want to do. Where there is love and inspiration, I don't think you can go wrong.
**Ella Fitzgerald**

I have accepted fear as part of life — specifically the fear of change. I have gone ahead despite the pounding in the heart that says: turn back.
**Erica Jong**

The doors we open and close each day decide the lives we live.
**Flora Whittemore**

I paint flowers so they will not die.
**Frida Kahlo**

Get comfortable with being uncomfortable!
**Jillian Michaels**

People, even more than things, have to be restored, renewed, revived, reclaimed, and redeemed; never throw out anyone.
**Audrey Hepburn**

It's really a wonder that I haven't dropped all my ideals, because they seem so absurd and impossible to carry out. Yet I keep them, because in spite of everything, I still believe that people are really good at heart.
**Anne Frank**

Whatever you want in life, other people are going to want too. Believe in yourself enough to accept the idea that you have an equal right to it.
**Diane Sawyer**

If my world were to cave in tomorrow, I would look back on all the pleasures, excitements and worthwhilenesses I have been lucky enough to have had. Not the sadness, not my miscarriages or my father leaving home, but the joy of everything else. It will have been enough. The best thing to hold onto in life is each other.
**Audrey Hepburn**

You must be the kind of man who can get things done. But to get things done, you must love the doing, not the secondary consequences.
**Ayn Rand**

Be more splendid, more extraordinary. Use every moment to fill yourself up.
**Oprah Winfrey**

Never give up, for that is just the place and time that the tide will turn.
**Harriet Beecher Stowe**

I hope the exit is joyful. And I hope never to return.
**Frida Kahlo**

Don't listen to other people's negativity: they filter through their own experiences. Learn to trust your own feelings.
**Ginger Purdy**

Without leaps of imagination, or dreaming, we lose the excitement of possibilities. Dreaming, after all, is a form of planning.
**Gloria Steinem**

Some people change when they see the light, others when they feel the heat.
**Caroline Schoeder**

Life is not easy for any of us. But what of that? We must have perseverance and above all confidence in ourselves. We must believe that we are gifted for something, and that this thing, at whatever cost, must be attained.
**Marie Curie**

Well, I hope that if you are out there and read this and know that, yes, it's true I'm here, and I'm just as strange as you.
**Frida Kahlo**

A friend is one who sees through you and still enjoys the view.
**Wilma Askinas**

Every great dream begins with a dreamer. Always remember, you have within you the strength, the patience, and the passion to reach for the stars to change the world.
**Harriet Tubman**

When we do the best that we can, we never know what miracle is wrought in our life, or in the life of another.
**Helen Keller**

Luck can only get you so far.
**J. K. Rowling**

From your parents you learn love and laughter and how to put one foot before the other but when books are opened you discover you have wings.
**Helen Hayes**

I pray every single second of my life; not on my knees but with my work. My prayer is to lift women to equality with men. Work and worship are one with me.
**Susan B. Anthony**

What we have once enjoyed we can never lose. All that we love deeply becomes a part of us.
**Helen Keller**

I think a lot, but I don't say much.
**Anne Frank**

Owning our story and loving ourselves through that process is the bravest think that we'll ever do.
**Brené Brown**

You may believe that you are responsible for what you do, but not for what you think. The truth is that you are responsible for what you think, because it is only at this level that you can exercise choice. What you do comes from what you think.
**Marianne Williamson**

Those of you who have the talent to do honor to poor womanhood, have all given yourself over to baby-making.
**Susan B. Anthony**

I believe in being strong when everything seems to be going wrong. I believe that happy girls are the prettiest girls. I believe that tomorrow is another day and I believe in miracles.
**Audrey Hepburn**

Have a bias toward action. Let's see something happen now. You can break that big plan into small steps and take the first step right way.
**Indira Gandhi**

I like the night. Without the dark, we'd never see the stars.
**Stephenie Meyer**

Far away there in the sunshine are my highest aspirations. I may not reach them, but I can look up and see their beauty, believe in them, and try to follow where they lead.
**Louisa May Alcott**

There's no human being who doesn't dream. We don't yet know why this plunge into dream-mind and its freedoms is needed, but we do know that imagination is as necessary as air.
**Jane Hirshfield**

Join the union, girls, and together say Equal Pay for Equal Work.
**Susan B. Anthony**

There will always be some curve balls in your life. Teach your children to thrive in that adversity.
**Jeanne Moutoussamy-Ashe**

Nothing destroys a good idea faster than a mandatory consensus.
**Jessica Hagy**

The weak fall, but the strong will remain and never go under!
**Anne Frank**

I am my own muse. I am the subject I know best. The subject I want to better.
**Frida Kahlo**

Some people thrive on huge, dramatic change. Some people prefer the slow and steady route. Do what's right for you.
**Julie Morgenstern**

You can look for external sources of motivation and that can catalyze a change, but it won't sustain one. It has to be from an internal desire.
**Jillian Michaels**

This is not the end. It is not even the beginning of the end. But it is, perhaps, the end of the beginning.
**Anne Frank**

Imagination is the highest kite that can fly.
**Lauren Bacall**

The cure for boredom is curiosity. There is no cure for curiosity.
**Ellen Parr**

Modern invention has banished the spinning wheel, and the same law of progress makes the woman of today a different woman from her grandmother.
**Susan B. Anthony**

Every day brings a choice: to practice stress or peace.
**Joan Borysenko**

Hope is the feeling that the feeling you have isn't permanent.
**Joan Kerr**

Whatever we are waiting for — peace of mind, contentment, grace, the inner awareness of simple abundance — it will surely come to us, but only when we are ready to receive it with an open and grateful heart.
**Sara Ban Breathnach**

Without dreams we couldn't live.
**Kara Melancon**

Healing takes courage, and we all have courage, even if we have to dig a little to find it.
**Tori Amos**

You must learn a new way to think before you can master a new way to be.
**Marianne Williamson**

Self-esteem must be earned! When you dare to dream, dare to follow that dream, dare to suffer through the pain, sacrifice, self-doubts and friction from the world, you will genuinely impress yourself.
**Laura Schlessinger**

Let your joy scream across the pain.
**Terri Guillemets**

But if you do believe, then you already know all about magic.
**Lauren Oliver**

The most important thing I have learned over the years is the difference between taking one's work seriously and taking one's self seriously. The first is imperative, and the second disastrous.
**Margot Fonteyn**

Sometimes good things fall apart, so better things can fall together.
**Marilyn Monroe**

I went to jail for eleven days for disturbing the peace. I was trying to disturb the war.
**Joan Baez**

If you don't like something, change it; if you can't change it, change the way you think about it.
**Mary Engelbreit**

We are each gifted in a unique and important way. It is our privilege and our adventure to discover our own special light.
**Mary Dunbar**

A mediocre idea that generates enthusiasm will go farther than a great idea that inspires no one.
**Mary Kay Ash**

The excitement of learning separates youth from old age. As long as you're learning, you're not old.
**Rosalyn S. Yalow**

My mission in life is not merely to survive, but to thrive; and to do so with some passion, some compassion, some humor, and some style.
**Maya Angelou**

Stress is an ignorant state. It believes that everything is an emergency. Nothing is that important.
**Natalie Goldberg**

I distrust those people who know so well what God wants them to do, because I notice it always coincides with their own desires.
**Susan B. Anthony**

Don't suffocate your spirit for the lessons that were only passing through spring.
**Nikki Rowe**

If you want to feel good, you have to go out and do some good.
**Oprah Winfrey**

Everybody has a list of 100 things they would like to change about themselves. But it's all about focusing on the good things.
**Taylor Swift**

You cannot make yourself feel something you do not feel, but you can make yourself do right in spite of your feelings.
**Pearl S. Buck**

Crazy is the price you pay for having an imagination. It's your superpower. Tapping into the dream. It's a good thing not a bad thing.
**Ruth Ozeki**

I try to make my mood uplifting and peaceful, then watch the world around me reflect that mood.
**Yaya DaCosta**

Choice is more than picking "x" over "y." It is a responsibility to separate the meaningful and the uplifting from the trivial and the disheartening. It is the only tool we have that enables us to go from who we are today to who we want to be tomorrow.
**Sheena Iyengar**

There is no history about which there is so much ignorance as this great movement for the establishment of equal political rights for women. I hope the twentieth century will see the triumph of our cause.
**Susan B. Anthony**

Don't waste your energy trying to change opinions. Do your thing and don't care if they like it.
**Tina Fey**

In this moment, there is plenty of time. In this moment, you are precisely as you should be. In this moment, there is infinite possibility.
**Victoria Moran**

One's philosophy is not best expressed in words; it is expressed in the choices one makes...and the choices we make are ultimately our responsibility.
**Eleanor Roosevelt**

Use what you've been through as fuel, believe in yourself and be unstoppable!
**Yvonne Pierre**

It is confidence in our bodies, minds, and spirts that allows us to keep looking for new adventures.
**Oprah Winfrey**

Love yourself and dream bigger.
**Teresa Collins**

You deserve the best, the very best, because you are one of the few people in this lousy world who are honest to themselves, and that is the only thing that really counts.
**Frida Kahlo**

CHAPTER 4

# Happiness

Happiness is the emotional state of a happy person; it is the feeling of well-being and fulfillment that we experience when we reach our goals, desires, and purposes. It is a lasting moment of satisfaction, where there are no pressing needs, nor tormenting sufferings.

Happiness is a subjective and relative condition. As such, there are no objective requirements to be happy: two people need not be happy for the same reasons or under the same conditions and circumstances.

In theory, the feeling of self-fulfillment and the fulfillment of our desires and aspirations are important aspects to feeling happy.

Most important, to be happy no precondition is necessary. Thus, there are people who are always happy and who feel comfortable with life and with what was given to them in grace. And, unfortunately, there are people who, despite having all the conditions to be well, regularly feel deeply unhappy.

For psychology, happiness is a positive emotional state that individuals reach when they have satisfied their desires and fulfilled their goals.

Happiness as such is measured by the ability of each person to provide solutions to the various aspects that make up their daily lives. In this sense, people who have these aspects covered should be happier, feel self-realized and full.

However, true happiness is something utopian, since it considers that for it to be possible, it would not depend on the real world, where individuals are constantly exposed to unpleasant experiences, such as failures and frustrations. In this sense, maintains that at the most what a human being could aspire to is only partial happiness.

For Aristotle, happiness was related to balance and harmony and was achieved through actions aimed at self-realization. Epicurus, for his part, pointed out that happiness was the satisfaction of desires and pleasures.

On the other hand, Chinese philosophers, like Lao-Tzu, pointed out that happiness could be achieved having nature as a model. While Confucius was of the opinion that happiness was given by the harmony between people.

Happiness depends on the glass through which you look, and on how and when you are willing to be happy with how much or how little you have.

For me, the most important thing will always be the people who are by our sides to share happiness with us.

---

*You won't be happy with more until you're happy with what you've got.*

Viki King

# Happiness Quotes

If you want your children to turn out well, spend twice as much time with them, and half as much money.
**Abigail Van Buren**

I have a simple philosophy: Fill what's empty. Empty what's full. And scratch where it itches.
**Alice Roosevelt Longworth**

Joy is strength.
**Mother Teresa**

No one's happiness but my own is in my power to achieve or to destroy.
**Ayn Rand**

The person who knows how to laugh at themselves will never cease to be amused.
**Shirley MacLaine**

Don't wait around for other people to be happy for you. Any happiness you get you've got to make yourself.
**Alice Walker**

Happiness is not a goal. It's a by-product of a life well lived.
**Eleanor Roosevelt**

In our work and in our living, we must recognize that difference is a reason for celebration and growth, rather than a reason for destruction.
**Audre Lorde**

The most important thing is to enjoy your life — to be happy — it's all that matters.
**Audrey Hepburn**

Self-worth is so vital to your happiness. If you don't feel good about YOU, it's hard to feel good about anything else.
**Mandy Hale**

The most beautiful people I've known are those who have known trials, have known struggles, have known loss, and have found their way out of the depths.
**Elisabeth Kübler-Ross**

Learn to value yourself, which means: fight for your happiness.
**Ayn Rand**

Power means happiness; power means hard work and sacrifice.
**Beyoncé**

Happiness also consists of what you let go, for your own good.
**Coco Chanel**

It's funny how the universe guides you to where you're meant to be. I wanted to make people Happy.
**Ellen DeGeneres**

Happiness arises in a state of peace, not of tumult.
**Ann Radcliffe**

Happiness is having somebody to share your swing set with.
**Crystal**, age 7, *Children on Happiness*

Happy people are beautiful. They become like a mirror and they reflect that happiness.
**Drew Barrymore**

Since you get more joy out of giving joy to others, you should put a good deal of thought into the happiness that you are able to give.
**Eleanor Roosevelt**

Remember that not to be happy is not to be grateful.
**Elizabeth Carter**

The greater part of our happiness or misery depends upon our dispositions, and not upon our circumstances.
**Martha Washington**

This isn't just "another day, another dollar." It's more like "another day, another miracle."
**Victoria Moran**

The greatest gift you can ever give another person is your own happiness.
**Esther Hicks**

Happiness is an attitude. We either make ourselves miserable, or happy and strong. The amount of work is the same.
**Francesca Reigler**

There can be no happiness if the things we believe in are different from the things we do.
**Freya Stark**

I've always loved journaling as a way to clear my mind. Whether I'm traveling or at home, the first thing I do when I wake up is pull out my notebook and record positive things that have happened to me as well as uplifting thoughts.
**Gloria Reuben**

The longest way must have its close — the gloomiest night will wear on to a morning.
**Harriet Beecher Stowe**

Many persons have a wrong idea of what constitutes true happiness. It is not attained through self-gratification, but through fidelity to a worthy purpose.
**Helen Keller**

Luck is not chance, it is toil. Fortune is expensive, smile is earned.
**Emily Dickinson**

Happiness is good health and a bad memory.
**Ingrid Bergman**

I never said I wanted a "happy life," but an interesting one. From separation and loss, I have learned a lot. We don't even know how strong we are until we are forced to bring that hidden strength forward.
**Isabel Allende**

Jobs fill your pocket, adventures fill your soul.
**Jaime Lyn Beatty**

The only truly happy people are children and the creative minority.
**Jean Caldwell**

Achievement of your happiness is the only moral purpose of your life, and that happiness, not pain or mindless self-indulgence, is the proof of your moral integrity, since it is the proof and the result of your loyalty to the achievement of your values.
**Ayn Rand**

Collect love everywhere you go.
**Jasmine**, age 9, *Children on Happiness*

Truth and confidence are the roots of happiness.
**Kathleen Pedersen**

Happiness is not a station you arrive at, but a manner of traveling.
**Margaret B. Runbeck**

Traveling is like flirting with life. It's like saying, "I would stay and love you, but I have to go; this is my station."
**Lisa St. Aubin de Terán**

One child, one teacher, one book, one pen can change the world.
**Malala Yousafzai**

An amazing thing happens when you stop seeking approval and validation: You find it. People are naturally drawn like magnets to those who know who they are and cannot be shaken!
**Mandy Hale**

Do things that make you happy within the confines of the legal system.
**Ellen DeGeneres**

A happy life consists not in the absence, but in the mastery of hardships.
**Helen Keller**

My idea of a good night has always been having a lovely meal and a proper conversation.
**Kirsty Gallacher**

Joy is the goal of existence, and joy is not to be stumbled upon, but to be achieved, and the act of treason is to let its vision drown in the swamp of the moment's torture.
**Ayn Rand**

When you are happy you can forgive a great deal.
**Princess Diana**

Being different is a revolving door in your life where secure people enter and insecure exit.
**Shannon L. Alder**

Happiness is an inside job. Don't assign anyone else that much power over your life.
**Mandy Hale**

I am determined to be cheerful and happy in whatever situation I may find myself. For I have learned that the greater part of our misery or unhappiness is determined not by our circumstance but by our disposition.
**Martha Washington**

If only we'd stop trying to be happy we'd have a pretty good time.
**Edith Wharton**

The true woman will not be exponent of another, or allow another to be such for her. She will be her own individual self. Stand or fall by her own individual wisdom and strength. She will proclaim the "glad tidings of good news" to all women, that woman equally with man was made for her own individual happiness, to develop every talent given to her by God, in the great work of life.
**Susan B. Anthony**

Creativity is inventing, experimenting, growing, taking risks, breaking rules, making mistakes, and having fun.
**Mary Lou Cook**

Be happy in the moment, that's enough. Each moment is all we need, not more.
**Mother Teresa**

It is the ultimate luxury to combine passion and contribution. It's also a very clear path to happiness.
**Sheryl Sandberg**

Even though you're growing up, you should never stop having fun.
**Nina Dobrev**

One of the keys to happiness is a bad memory.
**Rita Mae Brown**

Many people lose the small joys in the hope for the big happiness.
**Pearl S. Buck**

When you begin to touch your heart or let your heart be touched, you begin to discover that it's bottomless.
**Pema Chödrön**

I have been very happy with my homes, but homes really are no more than the people who live in them.
**Nancy Reagan**

For me, singing sad songs often has a way of healing a situation. It gets the hurt out in the open into the light, out of the darkness.
**Reba McEntire**

I hope you will understand my hesitation in writing to one whom I admire as the greatest representative of a philosophy to which I want to dedicate my whole life.
**Ayn Rand**

Be bold enough to live life on your terms, and never apologize for it.
**Mandy Hale**

You live longer once you realize that any time spent being unhappy is wasted.
**Ruth E. Renkl**

Today expect something good to happen to you no matter what occurred yesterday. Realize the past no longer holds you captive. It can only continue to hurt you if you hold on to it. Let the past go. A simply abundant world awaits.
**Sarah Ban Breathnach**

I have learned from experience that the greater part of our happiness or misery depends on our dispositions and not on our circumstances.
**Martha Washington**

I think of life itself now as a wonderful play that I've written for myself and so my purpose is to have the utmost fun playing my part.
**Shirley MacLaine**

The trees, the flowers, the plants grow in silence. The stars, the sun, the moon move in silence. Silence gives us a new perspective.
**Mother Teresa**

Mindfulness isn't difficult, we just need to remember to do it.
**Sharon Salzberg**

Independence is happiness.
**Susan B. Anthony**

I want to be the kind of person who can do that. Move on and forgive people and be healthy and happy. It seems like an easy thing to do in my head. But it's not so easy when you try it in real life.
**Susane Colasanti**

You were born an original work of art. Stay original always. Originals cost more than imitations.
**Suzy Kassem**

Give your stress wings and let it fly away.
**Terri Guillemets**

It stands to reason that anyone who learns to live well will die well. The skills are the same: being present in the moment, and humble, and brave, and keeping a sense of humor.
**Victoria Moran**

Life is the reward of virtue. And happiness is the goal and reward of life.
**Ayn Rand**

I will never understand all the good that a simple smile can accomplish.
**Mother Teresa**

That is happiness; to be dissolved into something complete and great.
**Willa Cather**

Can verbs be made up? I'll tell you one. I heaven you, so my wings will open wide to love you boundlessly. I am not sick. I am broken. But I am happy to be alive as long as I can paint.
**Frida Kahlo**

CHAPTER 5

# Life

The word life comes from the Latin *vita* and has several meanings.

Most of us think of life as the period from birth to death. Others view life as the existence and capacity of living things and beings to develop, reproduce, and maintain themselves within the earth's environment. Others see life as a spiritual or soulful journey, viewing humans as spiritual beings occupying the human body form.

How we approach our earthly existence determines our life experiences and our interpretations of these experiences. Is everything we experience a learning experience for our souls? Have we been here before and is this another reincarnation experience? Do we bring previous life experiences into our current journeys? What is the role of karma, pre-destination, luck, circumstance, or synchronicity?

Women and men throughout the ages have pondered these questions and many others. All have been inspired by the thinking and words of wisdom of their ancestors and those who have preceded them. One common thought throughout the ages: each of us is responsible for the quality of life that we personally experience.

We all know that life is precious, full of remarkable beauty, and something to enjoy. Unfortunately, in our hectic, 24/7, nonstop daily lives we often fail to stop and notice the bountiful beauties and joys of life surrounding us.

We also often fail to notice that as humans we have more in common with one another than our differences. Lately life around the world seems to be more focused on what divides us than what unites us. Women of today – and in future generations – need to be the central source unity all humanity and respecting all forms of life. Perhaps the quotations in this section will inspire you to become one such woman.

Having a purpose in life is often deemed a desirable trait. It means that you will focus your talents on something bigger than yourself. Or that you will use your unique skills, capabilities, and experiences to help others, on a local, national, or global scale. It also means that you will stop playing smaller than your potential.

Having a purpose in life helps you become someone with passion, someone with drive, someone with energy, and someone with commitment.

Theories and beliefs aside, we must always remember that life is present in everything around us: in the sun that warms us, in a sunset that awes us, in the laughter of a child, in the cry of a newborn baby, in an animal or pet that gets excited when we arrive home, in a freshly baked cake, in the wonderment of a starry sky, in a beautiful flower, in the sound of the sea, etc.

LIFE IS HERE AND NOW.

---

*Life's challenges are not supposed to paralyze you, they're supposed to help you discover who you are.*

Bernice Johnson Reagon

# Life Quotes

The purpose of our lives is to give birth to the best which is within us.
**Marianne Williamson**

There are two kinds of people in the world. Those who walk into a room and say "There you are" and those who say "Here I am."
**Abigail Van Buren**

My philosophy is that not only are you responsible for your life, but doing the best at this moment puts you in the best place for the next moment.
**Oprah Winfrey**

Life is an opportunity, benefit from it. Life is beauty, admire it. Life is a dream, realize it. Life is a challenge, meet it. Life is a duty, complete it. Life is a game, play it. Life is a promise, fulfill it. Life is sorrow, overcome it. Life is a song, sing it. Life is a struggle, accept it. Life is a tragedy, confront it. Life is an adventure, dare it. Life is luck, make it. Life is too precious, do not destroy it. Life is life, fight for it.
**Mother Teresa**

Life is what we make it, always has been, always will be.
**Grandma Moses**

Activism is the rent I pay for living on this planet.
**Alice Walker**

Creativity is not restricted to the arts. Creativity is an approach to living life.
**Alyce Cornyn-Selby**

The most difficult thing is the decision to act, the rest is merely tenacity.
**Amelia Earhart**

One's life has value so long as one attributes value to the life of others, by means of love, friendship and compassion.
**Simone de Beauvoir**

Music melts all the separate parts of our bodies together.
**Anaïs Nin**

If life were predictable it would cease to be life, and be without flavor.
**Eleanor Roosevelt**

The more you live, the less you die.
**Janis Joplin**

When it comes to human dignity, we cannot make compromises.
**Angela Merkel**

When you cease to make a contribution, you begin to die.
**Eleanor Roosevelt**

The thing that is really hard, and really amazing, is giving up on being perfect and beginning the work of becoming yourself.
**Anna Quindlen**

Class is an aura of confidence that is being sure without being cocky. Class has nothing to do with money. Class never runs scared. It is self-discipline and self-knowledge. It's the sure footedness that comes with having proved you can meet life.
**Ann Landers**

How wonderful it is that nobody need wait a single moment before starting to improve the world.
**Anne Frank**

Life is not easy for any of us. But what of that? We must have perseverance and above all confidence in ourselves.
**Marie Curie**

If I just think of how we live here, I usually come to the conclusion that it is a paradise compared with how other Jews who are not in hiding must be living.
**Anne Frank**

Old age is the verdict of life.
**Amelia E. Barr**

Perfectionism means that you try desperately not to leave so much mess to clean up, but clutter and mess show us that life is being lived.
**Anne Lamott**

Make no judgments where you have no compassion.
**Anne McCaffrey**

Good communication is as stimulating as black coffee, and just as hard to sleep after.
**Anne Morrow Lindbergh**

Reading is not just an escape. It is access to a better way of life.
**Karin Slaughter**

In this world of change, nothing which comes stays, nothing which goes is lost.
**Sophie Swetchine**

Sometimes the most urgent thing you can possibly do is take a complete rest.
**Ashleigh Brilliant**

Nothing is impossible, the word itself says "I'm possible!"
**Audrey Hepburn**

Don't wait for your feelings to change to take the action. Take the action and your feelings will change.
**Barbara Baron**

A problem clearly stated is a problem half solved.
**Dorothea Brande**

In order to experience everyday spirituality, we need to remember that we are spiritual beings spending some time in a human body.
**Barbara De Angelis**

Because true belonging only happens when we present our authentic, imperfect selves to the world, our sense of belonging can never be greater than our level of self-acceptance.
**Brené Brown**

It is important to use all knowledge ethically, humanely and lovingly.
**Carol Lynn Pearson**

As I see it every day you do one of two things: build health or produce disease in yourself.
**Adelle Davis**

We are each other's harvest; we are each other's business; we are each other's magnitude and bond.
**Gwendolyn Brooks**

And in life, it is all about choices we make. And how the direction of our lives comes down to the choices we choose.
**Catherine Pulsifer**

How we remember, what we remember and why we remember form the most personal map of our individuality.
**Christina Baldwin**

It's been said that there are two days over which we have no control: yesterday, because it's a cancelled check, and tomorrow, because it's a promissory note.
**Diane Conway**

You can be the ripest, juiciest peach in the world, and there are still going to be some people who hate peaches.
**Dita Von Teese**

As much research as you think you're doing, you're going to mess up, without a question.
**Doris Kearns Goodwin**

Some of the best days of your life haven't happened yet.
**Anne Frank**

Only when we are no longer afraid do we begin to live.
**Dorothy Thompson**

In every single thing you do, you are choosing a direction. Your life is a product of choices.
**Kathleen Hall**

In chaos, there is fertility.
**Anaïs Nin**

When we grow old, there can only be one regret — not to have given enough of ourselves.
**Eleonora Duse**

There is a way that nature speaks, that land speaks. Most of the time we are simply not patient enough, quiet enough, to pay attention to the story.
**Linda Hogan**

Enthusiasm is contagious. Be a carrier.
**Susan Rabin**

Don't follow the crowd, let the crowd follow you.
**Margaret Thatcher**

The most beautiful people we have known are those who have known defeat, known suffering, known struggle, known loss, and have found their way out of the depths. These persons have an appreciation, a sensitivity and an understanding of life that fills them with compassions, gentleness, and a deep loving concern. Beautiful people do not just happen.
**Elisabeth Kübler-Ross**

I've learned that making a "living" is not the same thing as "making" a life.
**Maya Angelou**

It's our challenges and obstacles that give us layers of depth and make us interesting. Are they fun when they happen? No. But they are what make us unique. And that's what I know for sure...I think.
**Ellen DeGeneres**

I see the world gradually being turned into a wilderness. I hear the ever-approaching thunder, which will destroy us too. I can feel the sufferings of millions and yet, if I look up into the heavens, I think that it will all come right.
**Anne Frank**

Age is not a handicap. Age is nothing but a number. It is how you use it.
**Ethel Payne**

Pain, pleasure and death are no more than a process for existence. The revolutionary struggle in this process is a doorway open to intelligence.
**Frida Kahlo**

I don't want to have lived in vain like most people. I want to be useful or bring enjoyment to all people, even those I've never met. I want to go on living even after my death!
**Anne Frank**

If the world were a logical place, men would ride side saddle.
**Rita Mae Brown**

Decide on what you think is right, and stick to it.
**George Eliot [Mary Ann Evans]**

Mistakes are part of the dues one pays for a full life.
**Sophia Loren**

About the only thing that comes to us without effort is old age.
**Gloria Pitzer**

Any man can be a father but it takes someone special to be a dad.
**Anne Geddes**

Walking is also an ambulation of mind.
**Gretel Ehrlich**

I praise loudly; I blame softly.
**Catherine the Second**

I can say what most conductors can't say — I never ran my train off the track and I never lost a passenger.
**Harriet Tubman**

Life is a daring adventure or it is nothing at all.
**Helen Keller**

My private measure of success is daily. If this were to be the last day of my life would I be content with it? To live in a harmonious balance of commitments and pleasures is what I strive for.
**Jane Rule**

If I had my life to live again, I'd make the same mistakes, only sooner.
**Tallulah Bankhead**

Beautiful young people are accidents of nature but beautiful old people are works of art.
**Eleanor Roosevelt**

Life is a series of sales situations and the answer is NO if you don't ask.
**Patricia Fripp**

Life is very tough. If you don't laugh, it's tough.
**Joan Rivers**

There is not one big cosmic meaning for all, there is only the meaning we each give to our life.
**Anaïs Nin**

Time engraves our faces with all the tears we have not shed.
**Natalie Clifford Barney**

Action is the antidote to despair.
**Joan Baez**

Every day brings a choice: to practice stress or peace.
**Joan Borysenko**

The elegance of honesty needs no adornment.
**Merry Browne**

Rock bottom became the solid foundation on which I rebuilt my life.
**J. K. Rowling**

Life is too precious to be spent in this weaving and unweaving of false impressions.
**George Eliot [Mary Ann Evans]**

Life is a choice — as is how you handle the pitfalls along its bumpy road.
**Julie Donner Andersen**

Life is change. Growth is optional. Choose wisely.
**Karen Kaiser Clark**

I am a vegetarian. So I avoid contributing to the major environmental damage that the meat industry creates. I hope that soon we can make sure that everything we do is earth-friendly.
**Joan Jett**

I am beginning to learn that it is the sweet, simple things of life which are the real ones after all.
**Laura Ingalls Wilder**

It is terrifying to see the rich having parties day and night while thousands and thousands of people are dying of hunger.
**Frida Kahlo**

Talent is distributed equally around the world. Opportunity is not.
**Leila Janah**

I get up in the morning and I really do feel that the world is my oyster, and I start that way, the same as I would if I were preparing to write a song: put a blank piece of paper up on the piano and you go for it.
**Lesley Gore**

Every time I think that I'm getting old, and gradually going to the grave, something else happens.
**Lillian Carter**

Life is not easy for any of us. But what of that? We must have perseverance and above all confidence in ourselves. We must believe that we are gifted for something and that this thing must be attained.
**Marie Curie**

If you surrender completely to the moments as they pass, you live more richly those moments.
**Anne Morrow Lindbergh**

I think music has the power to transform people, and in doing so, it has the power to transform situations — some large and some small.
**Joan Baez**

Our children are not going to be just our children. They are going to be other people's husbands and wives and the parents of our grandchildren.
**Mary S. Calderone**

Surviving is important, but thriving is elegant.
**Maya Angelou**

You have been told that real life is not like college, and you have been correctly informed. Real life is more like high school.
**Meryl Streep**

When you establish peace, when you establish love, when you establish kindness here (inside), you cannot act any other way to the outside world.
**Mimi Ikonn**

A life not lived for others is not a life.
**Mother Teresa**

A library is where ideas sleep between covers, waiting for you to discover them.
**Lois Ehlert**

Each time we re-read a book we get more out of it because we put more into it. A different person is reading it, and therefore it is a different book.
**Muriel Clark**

But as I got older I realized it wasn't just the dreaming and wishing that made the dreams possible. It was the doing.
**Nan S. Russell**

Don't be afraid of death; be afraid of an unlived life. You don't have to live forever; you just have to live.
**Natalie Babbitt**

Justice is like Nature — it is not without us as a fact; it is within us as a great yearning.
**George Eliot [Mary Ann Evans]**

There's no such thing as ruining your life. Life's a pretty resilient thing, it turns out.
**Sophie Kinsella**

Dismantle your wounds so you stop living your life by them.
**Nikki Rowe**

I've learned that you can't have everything, and do everything, at the same time.
**Oprah Winfrey**

When you focus on what might have been, it gets in the way of what can be.
**Patricia Fripp**

Adults are always asking little kids what they want to be when they grow up because they're looking for ideas.
**Paula Poundstone**

I don't eat junk foods and I don't think junk thoughts.
**Peace Pilgrim**

Cleaning your house while your kids are still growing up is like shoveling the walk before it stops snowing.
**Phyllis Diller**

A life of reaction is a life of slavery, intellectually and spiritually. One must strive for a life of action, not reaction.
**Rita Mae Brown**

There are two people in the world that are not likeable: a master and a slave.
**Nikki Giovanni**

It is a common delusion that you can make things better by talking about them.
**Rose Macauley**

Adversity precedes growth.
**Rosemarie Rossetti**

Life is short, and it is up to you to make it sweet.
**Sarah Louise Delany**

Done is better than perfect.
**Sheryl Sandberg**

What is an adult? A child blown up by age.
**Simone de Beauvoir**

From birth to age 18, a girl needs good parents, from 18 to 35 she needs good looks, from 35 to 55 she needs a good personality, and from 55 on she needs cash.
**Sophie Tucker**

A bird doesn't sing because it has an answer, it sings because it has a song.
**Maya Angelou**

If we would have new knowledge, we must get us a whole world of new questions.
**Susanne Langer**

We can have it all, but not at the same time.
**Patricia Fripp**

As you enter positions of trust and power, dream a little before you think.
**Toni Morrison**

There are years that ask questions and years that answer.
**Zora Neale Hurston**

What a wonderful life I've had! I only wish I'd realized it sooner.
**Sidonie-Gabrielle Colette**

And it is not worth leaving this world if you have given so much pleasure to life.
**Frida Kahlo**

CHAPTER 6

# Success

Success is the happy and satisfying result of life. I also consider that it is associated with triumph, or the achievement of victory, in something that we have faced at a certain moment. Many people also associate success with public recognition, fame or wealth. The beauty of life is that each one of us gets to interpret and define success for ourselves.

Of course, this also means the notion of success is subjective and relative. What for one person can be a success, for another may only be a consolation in the face of failure. In this sense, we can consider as a success any result that generates a feeling of fulfillment and well-being or, in short, happiness.

In this way, there are successes formally obtained and associated with our personal performance, be it in the professional or, academic areas, in which we work so hard for promotion or monetary increases. There are also personal successes, such as managing to establish our own company before the age of forty, buying your own home, traveling around the world, or raising a family.

Hence, success is also an intimate feeling that occurs within us when we achieve what we set out to do or what we never thought we would achieve. Thus, the personal success of daily life can be to prepare that grandmother's delicious recipe. Everyone can have a very different definition of success and they are all valid.

As such, the value of success in life is both in great efforts and small actions, in the will to overcome adversities, in the awareness of our skills and abilities, and in the desire to always be better and get ahead.

---

*Success is most often achieved by those who don't know that failure is inevitable.*

Coco Chanel

---

# Success Quotes

Great difficulties may be surmounted by patience and perseverance.
**Abigail Adams**

I love to see a young girl go out and grab the world by the lapels. Life's a bitch. You've got to go out and kick ass.
**Maya Angelou**

I alone cannot change the world, but I can cast a stone across the waters to create many ripples.
**Mother Teresa**

Achievement doesn't come from what we do, but from who we are.
**Marianne Williamson**

No matter what accomplishments you make, somebody helped you.
**Althea Gibson**

Success isn't about the end result, it's about what you learn along the way.
**Vera Wang**

It is failure that gives you the proper perspective on success.
**Ellen DeGeneres**

You can't always expect a certain result, but you can expect to do your best.
**Anita Hill**

It is not what you do for your children, but what you have taught them to do for themselves, that will make them successful human beings.
**Ann Landers**

Character cannot be developed in ease and quiet. Only through experience of trial and suffering can the soul be strengthened, ambition inspired, and success achieved.
**Helen Keller**

I wasn't afraid to fail. Something good always comes out of failure.
**Anne Baxter**

Invest in yourself, in your education. There's nothing better.
**Sylvia Porter**

What is done cannot be undone, but one can prevent it happening again.
**Anne Frank**

Searching for the truth is the noblest occupation of man; its publication is a duty.
**Madame de Staël**

Success is like reaching an important birthday and finding you're exactly the same.
**Audrey Hepburn**

The ladder of success is the best climbed by stepping on the rungs of opportunity.
**Ayn Rand**

Whatever you want to do, if you want to be great at it, you have to love it and be able to make sacrifices for it.
**Maya Angelou**

If you're able to be yourself, then you have no competition.
**Barbara Cook**

The worst part of success is trying to find someone who is happy for you.
**Bette Midler**

What did you learn today? What mistake did you make that taught you something? What did you try hard at today?
**Carol Dweck**

Concentrate, play your game, and don't be afraid to win.
**Louisa May Alcott**

The most successful entrepreneurs I know are optimistic. It's part of the job description.
**Caterina Fake**

If we don't change, we don't grow. If we don't grow, we aren't really living.
**Gail Sheehy**

Personal action is your pathway to success, even if it is a little bit at a time!
**Catherine Pulsifer**

I must admit that I personally measure success in terms of the contributions an individual makes to their fellow human beings.
**Margaret Mead**

It's how you deal with failure that determines how you achieve success.
**Charlotte Whitton**

You can't just sit there and wait for people to give you that golden dream. You've got to get out there and make it happen for yourself.
**Diana Ross**

Success is a state of mind. If you want success, start thinking of yourself as a success.
**Joyce Brothers**

Learn. Know what you didn't know before.
**Eileen Fisher**

Great minds discuss ideas; average minds discuss events; small minds discuss people.
**Eleanor Roosevelt**

My ideas usually come not at my desk writing but in the midst of living.
**Anaïs Nin**

When you take risks you learn that there will be times when you succeed and there will be times when you fail and both are equally important.
**Ellen DeGeneres**

Success is a great deodorant.
**Elizabeth Taylor**

When we give ourselves permission to fail, we, at the same time, give ourselves permission to excel.
**Eloise Ristad**

I never dreamt of success. I worked for it.
**Estée Lauder**

I attribute my success to this: I never gave or took any excuse.
**Florence Nightingale**

Pretend that every single person you meet has a sign around his or her neck that says, "Make me feel important." Not only will you succeed in sales, you will succeed in life.
**Mary Kay Ash**

If you want children to keep their feet on the ground, put some responsibility on their shoulders.
**Abigail Van Buren**

I think that little by little I'll be able to solve my problems and survive.
**Frida Kahlo**

Never quit. Never give up.
**Gabby Douglas**

Your success and happiness lies in you. Resolve to keep happy, and your joy and you shall form an invincible host against difficulties.
**Helen Keller**

You have to be first, different, or great.
**Loretta Lynn**

If you look at what you have in life, you'll always have more. If you look at what you don't have in life, you'll never have enough.
**Oprah Winfrey**

I can be changed by what happens to me. I am not reduced by it.
**Maya Angelou**

It is better to look ahead and prepare than to look back and regret.
**Jackie Joyner-Kersee**

Marriages, like careers, need constant nurturing. The secret of having it all is loving it all.
**Joyce Brothers**

Creative minds have always been known to survive any kind of bad training.
**Anna Freud**

Teaching is a wonderful way to learn.
**Carol Dweck**

A mediocre idea that generates enthusiasm will go further than a great idea that inspires no one.
**Mary Kay Ash**

Character is what emerges from all the little things you were too busy to do yesterday, but did anyway.
**Mignon McLaughlin**

You cannot have a positive life and a negative mind.
**Joyce Meyer**

Champions know there are no shortcuts to the top. They climb the mountain one step at a time. They have no use for helicopters.
**Judi Adler**

If you're never scared or embarrassed or hurt, it means you never take any chances.
**Julia Sorel**

When you're that successful, things have a momentum, and at a certain point you can't really tell whether you have created the momentum or it's creating you.
**Annie Lennox**

Find out what you like doing best, and get someone to pay you for it.
**Katharine Whitehorn**

Anything you to do to stretch yourself out of your comfort zone will ultimately enable you to take larger risks and grow.
**Leslie Evans**

If you don't go after what you want, you'll never have it. If you don't ask, the answer is always no. If you don't step forward, you're always in the same place.
**Nora Roberts**

Belief in oneself is one of the most important bricks in building any successful venture.
**Lydia M. Child**

It is more important to know where you are going than to get there quickly.
**Mabel Newcomer**

The person interested in success has to learn to view failure as a healthy, inevitable part of the process of getting to the top.
**Joyce Brothers**

The distance is nothing; it is only the first step that is difficult.
**Madame Marie du Deffand**

Believe in a child's power to succeed and they will succeed.
**Maggie Keyser**

What is success? I think it is a mixture of having a flair for the thing that you are doing; knowing that it is not enough, that you have got to have hard work and a certain sense of purpose.
**Margaret Thatcher**

It is too much to hope that I shall keep up my success. I don't ask for that. All I shall do is my best — and hope.
**Audrey Hepburn**

The greatest sign of success for a teacher is to be able to say, "The children are now working as if I did not exist."
**Maria Montessori**

We can always choose to perceive things differently. You can focus on what's wrong in your life, or you can focus on what's right.
**Marianne Williamson**

Feel the power that comes from focusing on what excites you.
**Oprah Winfrey**

I think the key is for women not to set any limits.
**Martina Navratilova**

Success doesn't come to you, you go to it.
**Marva Collins**

Give yourself something to work toward — constantly.
**Mary Kay Ash**

You do what you have to do, to do what you want to do.
**Patricia Fripp**

Life is my college. May I graduate well, and earn some honors.
**Louisa May Alcott**

There's nothing of any importance except how well you do your work.
**Ayn Rand**

When you know yourself you are empowered. When you accept yourself you are invincible.
**Tina Lifford**

What we really want to do is what we are really meant to do. When we do what we are meant to do, money comes to us, doors open for us, we feel useful, and the work we do feels like play to us.
**Julia Cameron**

If you have made mistakes, there is always another chance for you. You may have a fresh start any moment you choose. For this thing we call "Failure" is not the falling down, but the staying down.
**Mary Pickford**

Success is liking yourself, liking what you do, and liking how you do it.
**Maya Angelou**

I think the challenge is to take difficult and painful times and turn them into something beneficial, something that makes you grow.
**Michelle Akers**

Success isn't about how much money you make; it's about the difference you make in people's lives.
**Michelle Obama**

We, the unwilling, led by the unknowing, are doing the impossible for the ungrateful. We have done so much, for so long, with so little, we are now qualified to do anything with nothing.
**Mother Teresa**

Don't limit yourself. Many people limit themselves to what they think they can do. You can go as far as you mind lets you. What you believe, you can achieve.
**Mary Kay Ash**

Nothing is more revealing than movement.
**Martha Graham**

My mission in life is not merely to survive, but to thrive; and to do so with some passion, some compassion, some humor, and some style.
**Maya Angelou**

Part of being a champ is acting like a champ. You have to learn how to win and not run away when you lose.
**Nancy Kerrigan**

The way to bring about change is to be proactive and active.
**Octavia Spencer**

You know you are on the road to success if you would do your job and not be paid for it.
**Oprah Winfrey**

When nothing is sure, everything is possible.
**Margaret Drabble**

We know only too well that what we are doing is nothing more than a drop in the ocean. But if the drop were not there, the ocean would be missing something.
**Mother Teresa**

The future belongs to charismatic communicators who are technically competent.
**Patricia Fripp**

I am always more interested in what I am about to do than what I have already done.
**Rachel Carson**

To be successful, you don't have to change who you are; you have to become more of who you are.
**Sally Hogshead**

The two important things I did learn were that you are as powerful and strong as you allow yourself to be, and that the most difficult part of any endeavor is taking the first step, making the first decision.
**Robyn Davidson**

To succeed in life, you need three things: a wishbone, a backbone, and a funny bone.
**Reba McEntire**

The essential question is not "How busy are you?" but "What are you busy at?"
**Oprah Winfrey**

The first 30 seconds and the last 30 seconds have the most impact in a presentation.
**Patricia Fripp**

You can't break the rules until you know how to play the game.
**Ricki Lee Jones**

The smartest thing I ever did was to hire my weakness.
**Sara Blakely**

If you're offered a seat on a rocket ship, don't ask what seat! Just get on.
**Sheryl Sandberg**

If you have a goal in life that takes a lot of energy, that requires a lot of work, that incurs a great deal of interest and that is a challenge to you, you will always look forward to waking up to see what the new day brings.
**Susan Polis Schutz**

Invest in yourself, in your education. There's nothing better.
**Sylvia Porter**

A library is a gateway to others' minds, hearts, and lives.
**Tamora Pierce**

I think in terms of evolutions, not revolutions. Failure is not part of my vocabulary.
**Shelia Lirio Marcelo**

Some people say I have attitude — maybe I do. But I think you have to. You have to believe in yourself when no one else does — that makes you a winner right there.
**Venus Williams**

Think big, start small.
**Patricia Fripp**

The question isn't who is going to let me; it's who is going to stop me.
**Ayn Rand**

At the end of the day, we can endure much more than we think we can.
**Frida Kahlo**

CHAPTER 7

# Gratitude

Gratitude is an attitude of recognition for something that has been received, a benefit, a gesture or a favor. Gratitude is a positive emotion studied by traditional psychology, which expresses appreciation to another person from whom help was received.

Gratitude is a feeling that you experience when you receive support in a difficult circumstance, which leads to corresponding action of gratitude. It can be expressed with a simple oral statement of thanks, a smile, a thank you for a certain situation, or a note with expressions of appreciation for support, a phone call, a gift, a warm hug, a warm kiss.

Appreciation does not imply returning the favor with another similar action. Rather, it is remembering the other person's act of generosity. Gratitude weighs the friendliness of the gesture of the other, rather than the very usefulness of the favor or service received.

Appreciation or being grateful implies appreciating at all times what others do for us, being aware of their attitude and helping by creating a commitment of trust and reciprocity with them.

Gratitude is a value that distinguishes us as people, since we all need each other. Although we are not generous to get a reward, she comes alone when we choose the right path, the path of good. Recognizing your neighbor, thinking about her and her happiness surely brings us happiness back to ourselves.

When someone does something for us, that attitude or behavior generates enormous satisfaction, very pleasant and this triggers the feeling of gratitude, because they positively value the favor or benefit obtained.

Gratitude implies appreciating at all times what others do for us, being aware of their attitude and helping to create a commitment of trust and reciprocity with them.

Finally, these are just some of the benefits that the act of appreciation brings: It connects us with life. It contributes to happiness and optimism. It reduces dissatisfaction. It helps us adapt to circumstances. It improves mental and physical health. It increases self-esteem, confidence, and security.

Never stop being grateful, because life itself will pay you back in full, everything you do for her, and for others.

*Gratitude makes sense of our past,*
*brings peace for today,*
*and creates a vision for tomorrow.*

Melody Beattie

# Gratitude Quotes

I like living. I have sometimes been wildly, despairingly, acutely miserable, racked with sorrow, but through it all I still know quite certainly that just to be alive is a grand thing.
**Agatha Christie**

Feeling gratitude isn't born in us — it's something we are taught, and in turn, we teach our children.
**Joyce Brothers**

Kind words are short and easy to speak, but their echoes are truly endless.
**Mother Teresa**

When you make a world tolerable for yourself you make a world tolerable for others.
**Anaïs Nin**

We delight in the beauty of the butterfly, but rarely admit the changes it has gone through to achieve that beauty.
**Maya Angelou**

We often take for granted the very things that most deserve our gratitude.
**Cynthia Ozick**

The more grateful I am, the more beauty I see.
**Mary Davis**

When one door of happiness closes, another opens, but often we look so long at the closed door that we do not see the one that has been opened for us.
**Helen Keller**

My gratitude for good writing is unbounded; I'm grateful for it the way I'm grateful for the ocean.
**Anne Lamott**

One can never pay in gratitude; one can only pay "in kind" somewhere else in life.
**Anne Morrow Lindbergh**

We are all more blind to what we have than to what we have not.
**Audre Lorde**

For beautiful eyes, look for the good in others; for beautiful lips, speak only words of kindness; and for poise, walk with the knowledge that you are never alone.
**Audrey Hepburn**

Thanksgiving is a typically American holiday. The lavish meal is a symbol of the fact that abundant consumption is the result and reward of production.
**Ayn Rand**

To move freely you must be deeply rooted.
**Bella Lewitzky**

This is hard. This is fun.
**Carol Dweck**

The choices we make every minute of every day can contribute to making someone's life a little bit better or worse even without intending to.
**Chikamso Efobi**

Learn to get in touch with the silence within yourself and know that everything in this life has a purpose. There are no mistakes, no coincidences. All events are given to us to learn from.
**Elisabeth Kübler-Ross**

If you want the rainbow, you gotta put up with the rain.
**Dolly Parton**

You only live once, but if you do it right, once is enough.
**Mae West**

When you feel that you have reached the end and that you cannot go one step further, when life seems to be drained of al purpose: What a wonderful opportunity to start all over again, to turn over a new page.
**Eileen Caddy**

The more one does and sees and feels, the more one is able to do, and the more genuine may be one's appreciation of fundamental things like home, and love, and understanding companionship.
**Amelia Earhart**

The purpose of our lives is to give birth to the best that is in us. It is only through our own personal awakening that the world can be awakened. We cannot give what we do not have.
**Marianne Williamson**

Gratitude unlocks the fullness of life. It turns what we have into enough, and more. It turns denial into acceptance, chaos to order, confusion to clarity. It can turn a meal into a feast, a house into a home, a stranger into a friend.
**Melody Beattie**

It is strange that the years teach us patience; that the shorter our time left on this planet, the greater our capacity for waiting.
**Elizabeth Taylor**

We're all supposed to be different. I want so badly to encourage everyone to say, "Who Am I and How Do I Want to Live My Life."
**Ellen DeGeneres**

I am in agreement with everything my father taught me and nothing my mother taught me.
**Frida Kahlo**

Thank you is the best prayer that anyone could say. I say that one a lot. Thank you expresses extreme gratitude, humility, understanding.
**Alice Walker**

Silent gratitude isn't very much to anyone.
**Gertrude Stein**

If I ever seem to take you for granted, forgive me.
**Helen Fitzwalter-Read**

Sometimes the little things in life mean the most.
**Helen Hopkins**

No one has ever become poor by giving.
**Anne Frank**

Although the world is full of suffering, it is full also of the overcoming of it.
**Helen Keller**

The virtue involved in helping those one loves is not selflessness or sacrifice, but integrity.
**Ayn Rand**

I decided, very early on, just to accept life unconditionally; I never expected it to do anything special for me, yet I seemed to accomplish far more than I had ever hoped. Most of the time it just happened to me without my ever seeking it.
**Audrey Hepburn**

Life is full of unexpected and certainly unwanted twists and turns, but what makes us who we are is determined by the way we handle those situations. This is what separates us from those who achieve and those who allow others to control their fate.
**Jennifer Cruz**

I enjoy life when things are happening. I don't care if it's good things or bad things. That means you're alive.
**Joan Rivers**

What a pure blessing it was to have a bath in a tub alone in a room where all you had to do was pump the water, not tote buckets. Then all you had to do was pull out the cork, not tote more buckets to the back porch — that kind of thing is easy to take lightly until you don't have it.
**Nancy Turner**

The present is not a potential past; it is the moment of choice and action.
**Simone de Beauvoir**

I have come to believe that giving and receiving are really the same. Giving and receiving — not giving and taking.
**Joyce Grenfell**

A year from now you may wish you had started today.
**Karen Lamb**

Dead people receive more flowers than the living ones because regret is stronger than gratitude.
**Anne Frank**

We are taught you must blame your father, your sisters, your brothers, the school, the teachers — you can blame anyone but never blame yourself — it's never your fault. But it's always your fault, because if you wanted to change, you're the one who has got to change. It's as simple as that, isn't it?
**Katharine Hepburn**

I am beginning to learn that it is the sweet, simple things of life which are the real ones after all.
**Laura Ingalls Wilder**

I owe a debt of gratitude to two other living justices. Sandra Day O'Connor and Ruth Bader Ginsburg paved the way for me and so many other women in my generation. Their pioneering lives have created boundless possibilities for women in the law.
**Elena Kagan**

Appreciation can make a day — even change a life. Your willingness to put it into words is all that is necessary.
**Margaret Cousins**

If worry were an effective weight-loss program, women would be invisible.
**Nancy Drew**

There are as many life missions as there are people. We are all unique. We are all important.
**Janet Gallagher Nestor**

Acceptance. It is the one thing everyone longs for. The one thing everyone craves. To walk into a room and be greeted by everyone with hugs and smiles. And in that small passing moment, you truly know you're loved, needed, and accepted.
**Rena Harmon**

We must believe that we are gifted for something, and that this thing, at whatever cost, must be attained.
**Marie Curie**

Life's ups and downs provide windows of opportunity to determine your values and goals. Think of using all obstacles as stepping stones to build the life you want.
**Marsha Sinetar**

I sometimes wonder if anyone will ever understand what I mean, if anyone will ever overlook my ingratitude and not worry about whether or not I'm Jewish and merely see me as a teenager badly in need of some good, plain fun.
**Anne Frank**

In the final analysis there is no solution to man's progress but the day's honest work, the day's honest decisions, the day's generous utterances and the day's good deed.
**Clare Boothe Luce**

In the end, though, maybe we must all give up trying to pay back the people in this world who sustain our lives. In the end, maybe it's wiser to surrender before the miraculous scope of human generosity and to just keep saying thank you, forever and sincerely, for as long as we have voices.
**Elizabeth Gilbert**

Through the eyes of gratitude, everything is a miracle.
**Mary Davis**

When you give appreciation in order to get something it's manipulation and people can sense it. Appreciate genuinely.
**Marilyn Suttle**

I think a hero is any person really intent on making this a better place for all people.
**Maya Angelou**

It has been said that life has treated my harshly; and sometimes I have complained in my heart because many pleasures of human experience have been withheld from me...if much has been denied me, much, very much, has been given me.
**Helen Keller**

The person who gives with a smile is the best giver because God loves a cheerful giver.
**Mother Teresa**

Gratitude turns what we have into enough, and more. It turns denial into acceptance, chaos into order, confusion into clarity...it makes sense of our past, brings peace for today, and creates a vision for tomorrow.
**Melody Beattie**

Maybe being grateful means recognizing what you have for what it is. Appreciating small victories. Admiring the struggle it takes to simply be human. At the end of the day, the fact that we have the courage to still be standing is reason enough to celebrate.
**Meredith Grey**

As a child, I didn't know what I didn't have. I'm thankful for the challenges early on in my life because now I have a perspective on the world and kind of know what's important.
**America Ferrera**

The universe is always speaking to us...sending us little messages, causing coincidences and serendipities, reminding us to stop, to look around, to believe in something else, something more.
**Nancy Thayer**

The only chance women have for justice in this country is to violate the law, as I have done, and as I shall continue to do.
**Susan B. Anthony**

Cheers to a new year and another chance for us to get it right.
**Oprah Winfrey**

We have all the light we need. We just need to put it in practice.
**Peace Pilgrim**

Creativity is inventing, experimenting, growing, taking risks, breaking rules, making mistakes, and having fun.
**Mary Lou Cook**

I still miss those I loved who are no longer with me but I find I am grateful for having loved them. The gratitude has finally conquered the loss.
**Rita Mae Brown**

I want to thank you for the profound joy I've had in the in the thought of you.
**Rossie Allison**

I'm thankful that when I go to bed at night, that I have been myself that day. And, I have been myself all the days before that.
**Taylor Swift**

I want to thank my parents for raising me to have confidence that is somehow disproportionate with my looks and abilities. Well done. That is what all parents should do.
**Tina Fey**

Look at a day when you are supremely satisfied at the end. It's not a day when you lounge around doing nothing; it's when you've everything to do, and you've done it.
**Margaret Thatcher**

I think one of the turning points in my life came a few years ago. I started going to sleep at night just talking to myself saying, "You Are Perfect Just The Way You Are."
**Ellen DeGeneres**

Things must be felt with the heart.
**Helen Keller**

Your time is way too valuable to be wasting on people that can't accept who you are.
**Turcois Ominek**

Let gratitude be the pillow upon which you kneel to say your nightly prayer. And let faith be the bridge you build to overcome evil and welcome good.
**Maya Angelou**

What I wanted to express very clearly and intensely was that the reason these people had to invent or imagine heroes and gods is pure fear. Fear of life and fear of death.
**Frida Kahlo**

CHAPTER 8

# Truth

Truth is the correspondence between what we think or know with reality.

In this sense, the truth supposes the agreement between what we affirm with what is known, felt, or thought. Hence, the concept of truth also encompasses values such as honesty, sincerity, and openness.

Likewise, the truth refers to the real and effective existence of something, that is, to the concrete reality at the level of the facts.

On the other hand, as truth is that which judgment or proposition that cannot be rationally refuted. Truth is the opposite of falsehood or lying.

Saint Thomas Aquinas believed that truth was the intelligibility of being and the correlation of the mind with reality, while for Kant, truth was a logical perfection of knowledge.

Absolute truths are the ideas or propositions that are true for all cultures and all times. Absolute truths are those that we can attribute to nature and to certain phenomena or facts, which are fixed, invariable, and unalterable. They can also be attributed to some transcendent significance, such as those associated with divinity in certain religions.

Relative truths, in this sense, depend on principles or norms associated with the culture or time from which they are being considered. Hence, the truth of certain statements or propositions depends on how they are being viewed, from what time, culture and point of view.

The truth is another of the values, which depend on the glass through which we look at each other and always results from listening or knowing the two sides of the coin.

---

*The greatest problem in the world today is tolerance. Everyone is so intolerant of each other.*

Princess Diana

# Truth Quotes

The most common way people give up their power is by thinking they don't have any.
**Alice Walker**

We don't see things as they are, we see them as we are.
**Anaïs Nin**

Remember, no one can make you feel inferior without your consent.
**Eleanor Roosevelt**

Be thankful for what you have; you'll end up having more. If you concentrate on what you don't have, you will never, ever have enough.
**Oprah Winfrey**

Realize that if a door closed, it's because what was behind it wasn't meant for you.
**Mandy Hale**

Peace begins with a smile.
**Mother Teresa**

Make-up can only make you look pretty on the outside but it doesn't help if you're ugly on the inside. Unless you eat the make-up.
**Audrey Hepburn**

It is our choices that show what we truly are, far more than our abilities.
**J. K. Rowling**

The most difficult times for many of us are the ones we give ourselves.
**Pema Chödrön**

The man who does not value himself, cannot value anything or anyone.
**Ayn Rand**

You can't use up creativity. The more you use, the more you have.
**Maya Angelou**

Anyone can possess, anyone can profess, but it is an altogether different thing to confess.
**Shannon L. Alder**

Many receive advice, only the wise profit from it.
**Harper Lee**

Until you make peace with who you are, you will never be content with what you have.
**Doris Mortman**

Love is what we were born with. Fear is what we learned here.
**Marianne Williamson**

In every single thing you do, you are choosing a direction. Your life is a product of choices.
**Kathleen Hall**

Beyond anything else, listen to yourself. You are meant to discover reality from inside and to direct your life in this way. As you begin to live according to your own guidance and your own daring, everything changes completely.
**Barbara Marciniak**

Change is not only likely, it's inevitable.
**Barbara Sher**

You may be disappointed if you fail, but you are doomed if you don't try.
**Beverly Sills**

Becoming is better than being.
**Carol Dweck**

I can be a better me than anyone can.
**Diana Ross**

Life is ten percent what you experience and ninety percent how you respond to it.
**Dorothy M. Neddermeyer**

Practice is the hardest part of learning, and training is the essence of transformation.
**Ann Voskamp**

Never worry about numbers. Help one person at a time and always start with the person nearest you.
**Mother Teresa**

There are two things people want more than sex and money…recognition and praise.
**Mary Kay Ash**

Do what you feel in your heart to be right — for you'll be criticized anyway. You'll be damned if you do, and damned if you don't.
**Eleanor Roosevelt**

The truest greatness lies in being kind, the truest wisdom in a happy mind.
**Ella Wheeler Wilcox**

Take responsibility for yourself…because no one's going to take responsibility for you.
**Tyra Banks**

The most violent element in society is ignorance.
**Emma Goldman**

Advice is what we ask for when we already know the answer but wish we didn't.
**Erica Jong**

Change means that what was before wasn't perfect. People want things to be better.
**Esther Dyson**

Were there none who were discontented with what they have, the world would never reach anything better.
**Florence Nightingale**

If we don't change, we don't grow. If we don't grow, we aren't really living.
**Gail Sheehy**

The secret of joy is the mastery of pain.
**Anaïs Nin**

Good enough is the new perfect.
**Becky Beaupre Gillespie**

Change is inevitable. Growth is intentional.
**Glenda Cloud**

Beauty — in projection and perceiving — is 99.9 percent attitude.
**Mary Grey Livingston Mankin**

The true secret of giving advice is, after you have honestly given it, to be perfectly indifferent whether it is taken or not, and never persist in trying to set people right.
**Hannah Whitall Smith**

The only thing worse than being blind is having sight but no vision.
**Helen Keller**

If you want to see the true measure of a man, watch how he treats his inferiors, not his equals.
**J. K. Rowling**

Guilt is a rope that wears thin.
**Ayn Rand**

Don't blow off another's candle for it won't make yours shine brighter.
**Jaachynma N.E. Agu**

The best security blanket a child can have is parents who respect each other.
**Jane Blaustone**

Don't follow any advice, no matter how good, until you feel as deeply in your spirit as you think in your mind that the counsel is wise.
**Joan Rivers**

No man is good enough to govern any woman without her consent.
**Susan B. Anthony**

Sometimes you have to be alone to truly know your worth.
**Karen A. Baquiran**

Yesterday is a cancelled check; tomorrow is a promissory note; today is the only cash you have — so spend it wisely.
**Kay Lyons**

Remember always that you not only have the right to be an individual, you have an obligation to be one.
**Eleanor Roosevelt**

If only our great thinkers could learn to talk, and our great talkers could learn to think.
**Ashleigh Brilliant**

When you go out of your comfort zone and it works, there's nothing more satisfying.
**Kristen Wiig**

To think too long about doing a thing often becomes its undoing.
**Eva Young**

We live in the present, we dream of the future, we learn eternal truths from the past.
**Madame Chiang Kai-shek**

My work is about the establishment of trust. For someone to share their authenticity with me is a soul-to-soul thing. It's not a lens-to-soul thing.
**Lisa Kristine**

The best thing to spend on your children is your time.
**Louise Hart**

The great thing about getting older is that you don't lose all the other ages you've been.
**Madeleine L'Engle**

We learn our lessons; we get hurt; we want revenge. Then we realize that actually, happiness and forgiving people is the best revenge.
**Madonna**

True beauty is not related to what color your hair is or what color your eyes are. True beauty is about who you are as a human being, your principles, your moral compass.
**Ellen DeGeneres**

One of the best times for figuring out who you are and what you really want out of life? Right after a break-up.
**Mandy Hale**

It used to be about trying to do something. Now it's about trying to be someone.
**Margaret Thatcher**

You can avoid reality, but you cannot avoid the consequences of avoiding reality.
**Ayn Rand**

I have no riches but my thoughts, yet these are wealth enough for me.
**Sarah Josepha Hale**

No matter how difficult and painful it may be, nothing sounds as good to the soul as truth.
**Martha Beck**

Real glamour is based on femininity.
**Marilyn Monroe**

This a wonderful day. I've never seen this one before.
**Maya Angelou**

God doesn't care that I have a sandwich on Yom Kippur. He cares that I helped a blind man across the street.
**Joan Rivers**

Motherhood in all its guises and permutations is more art than science.
**Melinda M. Marshall**

One often learns more from ten days of agony than from ten years of contentment.
**Merle Shain**

I hate extremes of any kind.
**Margaret Thatcher**

The truth is not for all men but only for those who seek it.
**Ayn Rand**

What you spend years building may be destroyed overnight; build it anyway.
**Mother Teresa**

What the world needs now is for each of us to be who we truly are, and to bring our gifts into the world. Don't hold back any longer. Be Present. Be You. That is enough. Really it is.
**Nancy Bishop**

It is impossible to feel grateful and depressed in the same moment.
**Naomi Williams**

If you do not tell the truth about yourself you cannot tell it about other people.
**Virginia Woolf**

The problem with socialism is that you eventually run out of other people's money.
**Margaret Thatcher**

I trust that everything happens for a reason, even if we are not wise enough to see it.
**Oprah Winfrey**

I can do things you cannot, you can do things I cannot; together we can do great things.
**Mother Teresa**

Never argue with the inevitable.
**Patricia Fripp**

Even the rich are hungry for love, for being cared for, for being wanted, for having someone to call their own.
**Mother Teresa**

You cannot be fair to others without first being fair to yourself.
**Vera Nazarian**

Do you know that one of the great problems of our age is that we are governed by people who care more about feelings than they do about thoughts and ideas.
**Margaret Thatcher**

Nothing ever goes away until it has taught us what we need to know.
**Pema Chödrön**

You are the product of your own brainstorm.
**Rosemary Konner Steinbaum**

Man has no nobler function than to defend the truth.
**Ruth McKenney**

Parenting is an awesome task. It is my job as a professional to be sure that mothers, fathers and entire families see it also as the most rewarding one they have ever undertaken.
**Ruth W. Lubic**

Embrace what you don't know, especially in the beginning, because what you don't know can become your greatest asset. It ensures that you will absolutely be doing things different from everybody else.
**Sara Blakely**

One of the greatest diseases is to be nobody to anybody.
**Mother Teresa**

The sad truth is that excellence makes people nervous.
**Shana Alexander**

The basic difference between being assertive and being aggressive is how our words and behavior affect the rights and wellbeing of others.
**Sharon Anthony Bower**

The way you treat yourself sets the standard for others.
**Sonya Friedman**

The biggest disease today is not leprosy or tuberculosis, but rather the feeling of being unwanted.
**Mother Teresa**

The truth was, he now belonged only to my past, and it was time I begin to accept it, as much as it hurt to do so.
**Tammara Webber**

A person's world is only as big as their heart.
**Tanya A. Moore**

There are no mistakes, only opportunities.
**Tina Fey**

Real integrity is doing the right thing, knowing that nobody's going to know whether you did it or not.
**Oprah Winfrey**

You came to this planet to be remarkable.
**Victoria Moran**

I am that clumsy human, always loving, loving, loving. And loving. And never leaving.
**Frida Kahlo**

CHAPTER 9

# Values

Values is a broad concept that can refer to a personal quality, virtue, or talent; to the importance, price, or the utility of something, as well as to a good or to the validity of a thing.

Why is it so important to have values? Because values are what give meaning to our life. Human values demonstrate the kind of person we are. Today, it seems that our societies' in which we live increasingly suffer from misplaced values, with too many people giving more importance to selfishness, self-interest and indifference.

In philosophy, the concept of value is related to the quality that some realities have when they are considered and estimated as good in a moral sense.

Maintaining the values that authenticate and dignify humanity is a source of satisfaction and fulfillment that marks and leaves its imprint wherever we go, earning in turn the respect of everyone who crosses our path.

Values can be attributed to a person or collectively to a society. Personal and societal values often determine how people and groups behave. As such, values are studied by a branch of philosophy known as axiology.

Trust, respect, honesty are examples of very well held values in a person.

As some studies say, values become guidelines that set the standards for consistent behavior. They become ideals, indicators of the way forward.

In this way, values allow us to find meaning in what we do, make the relevant decisions, take responsibility for our actions, and accept their consequences. They allow each of us to clearly define the goals of our lives. Values help us to accept ourselves as we are and to appreciate and love ourselves. Values also help us understand, cherish, and respect others. They facilitate a mature and balanced relationship with the environment and people, providing us with a powerful feeling of personal harmony.

*Sometimes the biggest act of courage is a small one.*

Lauren Raffo

# Values Quotes

Courage is the price that life exacts for granting peace. The soul that knows it not, knows no release from little things.
**Amelia Earhart**

Without courage we cannot practice any other virtue with consistency.
**Maya Angelou**

Don't be afraid your life will end; be afraid that it will never begin.
**Grace Hansen**

A woman is like a tea bag. You never know how strong she is until she gets into hot water.
**Eleanor Roosevelt**

Where there is no struggle, there is no strength.
**Oprah Winfrey**

I was always looking outside myself for strength and confidence but it comes from within. It is there all the time.
**Anna Freud**

Follow your passion. Stay true to yourself. Never follow someone else's path unless you're in the woods and you're lost and you see a path. By all means, you should follow that.
**Ellen DeGeneres**

If you want to change attitudes, start with a change in behavior.
**Katharine Hepburn**

I can shake off everything as I write; my sorrows disappear, my courage is reborn.
**Anne Frank**

Champions keep playing until they get it right.
**Billie Jean King**

Don't limit yourself. Many people limit themselves to what they think they can do.
**Mary Kay Ash**

A desire presupposes the possibility of action to achieve it; action presupposes a goal which is worth achieving.
**Ayn Rand**

I tried to drown my sorrows, but the bastards learned how to swim, and now I am overwhelmed by this decent and good feeling.
**Frida Kahlo**

We need to find the courage to say no to the things and people that are not serving us if we want to rediscover ourselves and live our lives with authenticity.
**Barbara De Angelis**

No matter who you are, no matter what you did, no matter where you've come from, you can always change, become a better version of yourself.
**Madonna**

Courage starts with showing up and letting ourselves be seen.
**Brené Brown**

I discovered I always have choices and sometimes it's only a choice of attitude.
**Judith M. Knowlton**

The soul always knows what to do to heal itself. The challenge is to silence the mind.
**Caroline Myss**

I beg you take courage; the brave soul can mend even disaster.
**Catherine the Great**

Life presents many choices, the choices we make determine our future.
**Catherine Pulsifer**

We gain strength, and courage, and confidence by each experience in which we really stop to look fear in the face…we must do that which we think we cannot.
**Eleanor Roosevelt**

Do you have the courage to bring forth the treasures that are hidden within you?
**Elizabeth Gilbert**

Light tomorrow with today!
**Elizabeth Barrett Browning**

Fear is inevitable. I have to accept that, but I cannot allow it to paralyze me.
**Isabel Allende**

When people already know they're deficient, they have nothing to lose by trying.
**Carol Dweck**

Though you feel like you're not where you're supposed to be, you shouldn't worry because the next turn you take, it will lead you to where you wanna go.
**Ellen DeGeneres**

Decide whether or not the goal is worth the risks involved. If it is, stop worrying.
**Amelia Earhart**

Sometimes the hardest part isn't letting go but rather learning to start over.
**Nicole Sobon**

It takes a lot of courage to show your dreams to someone else.
**Erma Bombeck**

I was a child who went about in a world of colors. My friends, my companions became women slowly; I became old in instants.
**Frida Kahlo**

Having courage does not mean we are unafraid.
**Maya Angelou**

Patience is the ability to idle your motor when you feel like stripping your gears.
**Barbara Johnson**

You have to accept whatever comes and the only important thing is that you meet it with courage and with the best that you have to give.
**Eleanor Roosevelt**

Just remember, you can do anything you set your mind to, but it takes action, perseverance and facing your fears.
**Gillian Anderson**

We aren't allowed to have any opinions. People can tell you to keep your mouth shut, but it doesn't stop you having your own opinion. Even if people are still very young, they shouldn't be prevented from saying what they think.
**Anne Frank**

If you are lucky enough to find a way of life you love, you have to find the courage to live it.
**Bette Davis**

I've finally stopped running away from myself. Who else is there better to be?
**Goldie Hawn**

Be of good cheer. Do not think of today's failures, but of the success that may come tomorrow. You have set yourselves a difficult task, but you will succeed if you persevere; and you will find a joy in overcoming obstacles.
**Helen Keller**

I find that it is not the circumstances in which we are placed, but the spirit in which we face them, that constitutes our comfort.
**Elizabeth T. King**

Something happens to me when I witness someone's courage. They may not know I'm watching and I might not let them know. But something happens to me that will last me for a lifetime; to fill me when I'm empty, and rock me when I'm low.
**Holly Near**

When you're different, sometimes you don't see the millions of people who accept you for what you are. All you notice is the person who doesn't.
**Jodi Picoult**

What made something precious? Losing it and finding it.
**Celeste Ng**

Unless you know what you want, you can't ask for it.
**Emma Albani**

My definition of courage is never letting anyone define you.
**Jenna Jameson**

Courage is the most important of all the virtues, because without courage you can't practice any other virtue consistently. You can practice any virtue erratically, but nothing consistently without courage.
**Maya Angelou**

Painting completed my life. I lost three children and a series of other things that would have fulfilled my horrible life. My painting took the place of all of this. I think work is the best.
**Frida Kahlo**

Nobody talks of entrepreneurship as survival, but that's exactly what it is.
**Anita Roddick**

Make it a rule of life never to regret. Regret is an appalling waste of energy — you can't build on it; it's only for wallowing in.
**Katherine Mansfield**

Real education should educate us out of self into something far finer; into a selflessness that links us with all humanity.
**Lady Nancy Astor**

The only courage that matters is the kind that gets you from one moment to the next.
**Mignon McLaughlin**

I think laughter may be a form of courage. As humans we sometimes stand tall and look into the sun and laugh, and I think we are never more brave than when we do that.
**Linda Ellerbee**

If you don't have the information you need to make wise choices, find someone who does.
**Lori Hil**

I am not afraid of storms, for I am learning how to sail my ship.
**Louisa May Alcott**

We are all just doing the best we know how with the understanding, awareness, and knowledge we have at the time.
**Louise L. Hay**

I must fight with all my strength so that the little positive things that my health allows me to do might be pointed toward helping the revolution. The only real reason for living.
**Frida Kahlo**

I was smart enough to go through any door that opened.
**Joan Rivers**

One of the things I learned the hard way was that it doesn't pay to get discouraged. Keeping busy and making optimism a way of life can restore your faith in yourself.
**Lucille Ball**

Don't let compliments get to your head and don't let criticism get to your heart.
**Lysa TerKeurst**

Only make decisions that support your self-image, self-esteem, and self-worth.
**Oprah Winfrey**

When nothing is sure, everything is possible.
**Margaret Drabble**

I don't want to die as long as I can work; the minute I cannot, I want to go.
**Susan B. Anthony**

There's always a point where you get knocked down. But I draw on what I've learned on the track: If you work hard, things will work out.
**Lolo Jones**

Pain nourishes courage. You can't be brave if you've only had wonderful things happen to you.
**Mary Tyler Moore**

You may have to fight a battle more than once to win it.
**Margaret Thatcher**

Knowing what must be done does away with fear.
**Rosa Parks**

To have character is to be big enough to take life on.
**Mary Caroline Richards**

If you don't like something, change it. If you can't change it, change your attitude. Don't complain.
**Maya Angelou**

Anything may be betrayed, anyone may be forgiven, but not those who lack the courage of their own greatness.
**Ayn Rand**

Sometimes one has simply to endure a period of depression for what it may hold of illumination.
**May Sarton**

People who are truly strong lift others up. People who are truly powerful bring others together.
**Michelle Obama**

Courage can't see around corners but goes around them anyway.
**Mignon McLaughlin**

I'm selfish, impatient and a little insecure. I make mistakes, I am out of control and at times hard to handle. But if you can't handle me at my worst, then you sure as hell don't deserve me at my best.
**Marilyn Monroe**

Don't let hollow heroes distract you from saving yourself.
**Nikki Rowe**

As you become more clear about who you really are, you'll be better able to decide what is best for you the first time around.
**Oprah Winfrey**

Every political leader worth their salt in history — from Gandhi to Martin Luther King — has expressed the same message, which is courage. Real leaders don't tell people to be frightened. They help people find a place of courage, even in the face of very real threats.
**Naomi Klein**

Eventually you just have to realize that you're living for an audience of one. I'm not here for anyone else's approval.
**Pamela Anderson**

I think we all have empathy. We may not have enough courage to display it.
**Maya Angelou**

What does it take to be a champion? Desire, dedication, determination, concentration, and the will to win.
**Patty Berg**

To uncover your true potential you must first find your own limits, and then you have to have the courage to blow past them.
**Picabo Street**

Some attributes of leadership are universal and are often about finding ways of encouraging people to combine their efforts, their talents, their insights, their enthusiasm, and their inspiration to work together.
**Queen Elizabeth II**

The older I get, the greater power I seem to have to help the world; I am like a snowball — the further I am rolled the more I gain.
**Susan B. Anthony**

Acceptance. It is the true thing everyone longs for. The one thing everyone craves. To walk in a room and to be greeted by everyone with hugs and smiles. And in that small passing moment, you truly know you're loved, needed and accepted.
**Rena Harmon**

Man has no nobler function than to defend the truth.
**Ruth McKenney**

Let the barriers you face — and there will be barriers — be external, not internal.
**Sheryl Sandberg**

Sometimes you don't realize your own strength until you come face to face with your greatest weakness.
**Susan Gale**

Don't live down to expectations. Go out there and do something remarkable.
**Wendy Wasserstein**

Resign yourself to the lifelong sadness that comes from never being satisfied.
**Zadie Smith**

At the end of the day, we can endure much more than we think we can.
**Frida Kahlo**

CHAPTER 10

# Forgiveness

Forgiveness is another critical human value. Forgiveness can serve, on the one hand, to enable the offender to free herself from guilt and, on the other hand, to free the offended from possible feelings of rancor. Forgiveness does not always mean that the offender does not have to make up for his mistake in some other way.

Knowing how to forgive is of immense personal value. So, too, is knowing how to ask for forgiveness, because doing so implies recognizing the guilt and the damage done to the other person. In Psychology, both actions are considered human capacities, which also tend to have very positive and liberating therapeutic effects.

Forgiveness is the action and the result of forgiving. You can forgive, among other things, an offense, a penalty, or a debt. It is also the indulgence or remission of certain sins that the human being can commit.

Asking for forgiveness is equivalent to apologizing. It is a generic concept since it can be applied in different contexts. You can ask for forgiveness from a person, a group, an institution, or a divinity.

Forgiveness is a noble act that every human being should humbly put into practice.

Asking for forgiveness is usually associated with acknowledging that an error has been made. Doing so usually shows that a person has an intention to rectify or compensate, in some way, for that error.

It is an act that, regardless of the power, fame, money, or position that a person has, must assume it and face it to rectify their lack and thus perceive how gratifying it feels to make a wrong decision, ask for forgiveness.

Finally, these are some of the benefits that the act of forgiveness brings:

- Healthier relationships
- Better mental health
- Less anxiety, stress and hostility
- Reduced blood pressure
- Fewer symptoms of depression
- Better heart health
- Increased self-esteem

*Forgiveness is the key to action and freedom.*

Hannah Arendt

# Forgiveness Quotes

The heart stays heavy if it remains in a state of unforgiveness.
**Aisha Mirza**

Forgiveness is a virtue of the brave.
**Indira Gandhi**

Genuine forgiveness does not deny anger but faces it head-on.
**Alice Duer Miller**

Forgiveness is not always easy. At times it feels more painful than the wound we suffered, to forgive the one that inflicted it. And yet, there is no peace without forgiveness.
**Marianne Williamson**

It's one of the greatest gifts you can give yourself, to forgive. Forgive everybody.
**Maya Angelou**

If we really want to love we must learn how to forgive.
**Mother Teresa**

Forgiveness is the economy of the heart. Forgiveness saves the expense of anger, the cost of hatred, the waste of spirits.
**Hannah More**

Forgiveness means it finally becomes unimportant that you hit back.
**Anne Lamott**

Before we can forgive one another, we have to understand one another.
**Emma Goldman**

Listen. Slide the weight from your shoulders and move forward. You are afraid that you might forget, but you never will. You will forgive and remember.
**Barbara Kingsolver**

I have learned that sometimes "sorry" is not enough. Sometimes you actually have to change.
**Claire London**

As long as you don't forgive, who and whatever it is will occupy a rent-free space in your mind.
**Isabelle Holland**

We don't forgive people because they deserve it. We forgive them because they need it — because we need it.
**Bree Despain**

By far the strongest poison to the human spirit is the inability to forgive oneself or another person. Forgiveness is no longer an option but a necessity for healing.
**Caroline Myss**

The forgiving state of mind is a magnetic power for attracting good.
**Catherine Ponder**

The practice of forgiveness is our most important contribution to the healing of the world.
**Marianne Williamson**

When you hold resentment toward another, you are bound to that person or condition by an emotional link that is stronger than steel. Forgiveness is the only way to dissolve that link and get free.
**Katherine Ponder**

Sometimes you just have to regret things and move on.
**Charlaine Harris**

Forgiving is easier when we understand that forgiving someone else means that we are freeing ourselves of an unnecessary burden.
**Donna Goddard**

How much bondage and suffering a woman escapes when she takes the liberty of being her own physician of both body and soul.
**Elizabeth Cady Stanton**

I'm a good enough person to forgive you, and you should be a good enough person to not do it again.
**Annette Thomas**

I learned compassion from being discriminated against. Everything bad that's ever happened to me has taught me compassion.
**Ellen DeGeneres**

Mistakes are part of the dues one pays for a full life.
**Sophia Loren**

There will always be a reason why you meet people. Either you need them to change your life or you're the one that will change theirs.
**Angel Flonis Harefa**

We mostly spend our lives conjugating three verbs: to Want, to Have, and to Do…forgetting that none of these verbs have any ultimate significance, except so far as they are transcended by and included in, the fundamental verb, to Be.
**Evelyn Underhill**

My painting carries with it the message of pain.
**Frida Kahlo**

I think we learn the most from imperfect relationships — things like forgiveness and compassion.
**Andrea Thompson**

You cannot forgive just once, forgiveness is a daily practice.
**Sonia Rumzi**

For me, forgiveness and compassion are always linked: how do we hold people accountable for wrongdoing and yet at the same time remain in touch with their humanity enough to believe in their capacity to be transformed.
**Bell Hooks**

Forgive me. Forgive this fool. Sorry that I acted so cruel. I love you and love only you. Take my hand and let's start anew.
**Gabrielle Yana Concepcion**

Life is accepting what is and working from that.
**Gloria Naylor**

You have been criticizing yourself for years, and it hasn't worked. Try approving of yourself and see what happens.
**Louise L. Hay**

Forgive all who have offended you, not for them, but for yourself.
**Harriet Nelson**

Forgiveness is giving up the hope that the past could have been any different.
**Oprah Winfrey**

For every lie I unlearn I learn something new.
**Ani DiFranco**

In the long run, we shape our lives, and we shape ourselves. The process never ends until we die and the choices we make are ultimately our own responsibility.
**Eleanor Roosevelt**

You can't shake hands with a clenched fist.
**Indira Gandhi**

Everybody has losses — it's unavoidable in life. Sharing our pain is very healing.
**Isabel Allende**

Being forgiven is like having all the worst bits of yourself stuffed into a balloon and then having that balloon set free.
**Shannon Wiersbitzky**

It is impossible to live without failing at something, unless you live so cautiously that you might as well not have lived at all, in which case you have failed by default.
**J. K. Rowling**

Love is an endless act of forgiveness.
**Jan Karon**

I can forgive almost anything. But let me be clear: forgiving and excusing are not the same thing.
**Michelle R. Gould**

Sometimes what a person needs most is to be forgiven.
**Jennifer McMahon**

Three months ago, if you asked me, I would have told you that if you really loved someone, you'd let them go. But now I look at you, and I dreamed about Maggie, and I see that I've been wrong. If you really love someone, Allie, I think you take them back.
**Jodi Picoult**

All that separates, whether of race, class, creed, or sex, is inhuman, and must be overcome.
**Kate Sheppard**

In any free society, the conflict between social conformity and individual liberty is permanent, irresolvable and necessary.
**Kathleen Norris**

I'm not perfect. Remember that, and try to forgive me when I fail you.
**Elizabeth Lowell**

Forgiving men is so much easier than forgiving women.
**Margaret Atwood**

Don't be defined by your past, your past is the tutor of your present and is always preparing you for new experience. Forget about disappointment or any past mistakes that is keeping you from moving forward. It's never too late for a new beginning.
**Kemmy Nola**

I cannot believe that war is the best solution. No one won the last war and no one will win the next.
**Eleanor Roosevelt**

When one has been threatened with a great injustice, one accepts a smaller as a favor.
**Jane Welsh Carlyle**

Anger, resentment, and jealousy doesn't change the heart of others — it only changes yours.
**Shannon L. Alder**

Like a loving spouse who occasionally doesn't feel so loving, we ask for forgiveness and come back into relationship.
**Laurie Penner**

We cannot always control our thoughts, but we can control our words, and repetition impresses the subconscious, and we are then master of the situation.
**Jane Fonda**

Forgiveness is not to give the other person peace. Forgiveness is for you. Take that opportunity.
**Mackenzie Phillips**

We are all on a life long journey and the core of its meaning, the terrible demand of its centrality is forgiving and being forgiven.
**Martha Kilpatrick**

You can't forgive without loving. And I don't mean sentimentality. I don't mean mush. I mean having enough courage to stand up and say, "I forgive. I'm finished with it."
**Maya Angelou**

In some families, please is described as the magic word. In our house, however, it was sorry.
**Margaret Laurence**

True forgiveness is when you can say, "Thank you for that experience."
**Oprah Winfrey**

It's toughest to forgive ourselves. So it's probably best to start with other people. It's almost like peeling an onion. Layer by layer, forgiving others, you really do get to the point where you can forgive yourself.
**Patty Duke**

I always feel sorry for people who think more about a rainy day ahead than sunshine today.
**Rae Foley**

Would "sorry" have made a difference? Does it ever? It's just a word. One word against a thousand actions.
**Sarah Ockler**

If you spend your time hoping someone will suffer the consequences for what they did to your heart, then you're allowing them to hurt you a second time in your mind.
**Shannon L. Alder**

Sometimes things have to go wrong in order to go right.
**Sherrilyn Kenyon**

Life beats down and crushes the soul and art reminds you that you have one.
**Stella Adler**

In love, everyone does things that hurt the other person, so there is really no "Right" and "Wrong." You just have to decide what you're willing to forgive.
**Yvonne Wood**

If you didn't love him, this never would have happened. But you did. And accepting that love and everything that followed it is part of letting it go.
**Sarah Dessen**

Forgiveness is not always easy. At times, it feels more painful than the wound we suffered, to forgive the one that inflicted it. And yet, there is no peace without forgiveness.
**Marianne Williamson**

To mature is to learn to want beautiful, to miss in silence, to remember without hard feelings, and to forget slowly.
**Frida Kahlo**

# Adriana's Favorite Sayings

- My family is the best gift life could give me.
- When you ask nothing and they give everything, there it is.
- Always keep this phrase in mind...I want, I can, and I am able.
- For love you don't have to give up anything, not your friends, not your talent, not your tastes. Love adds, does not subtract
- When you feel that place is no longer your place...fly.
- There's nothing bad from which good doesn't come.
- Love is born by the small details and dies from the lack of them.
- Of all the things you're wearing, your attitude is the most important.
- Make peace with your past so you don't have conflicts with your present.
- A real man is one who seeks a thousand ways to fall in love every day, with the same woman.
- When you don't let go, you carry it. What you carry, it weighs on you. And what weights on you sinks you. Practice the art of letting go, and letting go.

- People think that being alone at home is loneliness. I call it absolute peace.

- The woman has only one defect, she does not recognize how valuable she is.

- The true maturity is to shut up, smile, turn around, and change paths. Because where ignorance speaks, intelligence is silent.

- He who leaves after a taste, a love, and a coffee does not understand how ephemeral life is.

- You laugh for a while with a friend and life resets you.

- Leaving some places is also taking care of yourself. To get away from some people is also to protect yourself. Closing some doors is also love.

- My dad always told me: strive, study, work because if one day you get married and a bad man touches you, you send him to hell and go ahead alone.

- When you take pleasure in solitude, it is difficult to get excited again with anyone.

- Behind every successful woman is herself encouraging her to move on.

- I like people who know how to be sun. Even when life is cloudy.

- An enterprising woman has the luxury of being with whom she wants and not with whom she touches.

- If you look taller with a heel, with self-love you will look immense.

- Sitting like Buddha, standing like Joan of Arc.
- The only impossible thing is what you don't try.
- When a woman knows where she is going, she has two options: accompany her or get out of her way.
- A wise man said:

    GIVE...but don't let them use it.

    LOVE...but don't let them abuse your heart.

    TRUST...but don't be naïve.

    LISTEN...but don't lose your own voice.
- Behind a happy woman, she finds herself fighting everything to keep herself that way.
- Make peace with your past, so it doesn't ruin your future.
- What others think of you is not your problem.
- The only person capable of making you happy is yourself.

# Acknowledgements

This book would not have been possible without the inspiration of several very important women in my life such as: my sister, friend, and confidante Amelia.

My Aunt Palle who with her discretion, family focus, and integrity have been a great example for me to follow. Martha for her love and unconditional support. My cousins Ana Paula and Ceci.

My "sisters in life" Oriana, Annie, Silvia, Kata, Carolina, María Amparo, Ileana, and María Antonieta. With each of them I carry priceless memories in my heart and wonderful and unforgettable experiences.

To my first great boss and friend Beatriz Resler and my Colombian friends and colleagues that I greatly appreciate, value, and admire: Carol, Mafe, and Ayda.

A special thanks to Héctor Castañeda for the excellent work in the design of this book cover and to my dear friend and great artist Berenice Lacroix, who created this beautiful work of art for the book.

I also want to thank a few important men who have been very meaningful to me through all my life.

First, my two fathers Arturo and Beto for their unconditional support, love, dedication, advice, and guidance in the 45 short years of my life. And to my dear brother Carlos with whom I have shared so much since childhood.

To Enrique, my best boss and unconditional friend. For over 25 years, we continue to maintain a unique and exceptional friendship.

Paco Partida, another great boss and friend, who believes in my professional potential and is a great human being.

And lastly, for the two very special men in my life. To Steven, for magically appearing in my life and changing it in a romantically different and special way. I am grateful for having you in my life. This book would not have been possible without your help and support from start to finish.

And finally, my most precious treasure, my great engine and motivation for my life, and my reason for being and existing, my son ALFONSO.

# About the Author

Adriana Fuentes Díaz was born in Mexico City, spent most of her childhood and early adult years in Venezuela, and return to her city of birth seven years ago. She also lived in Newark, Delaware for a year as high school Exchange Student with a wonderful family.

After graduating with a degree in Communication and Advertising in Venezuela, Adriana studied Public Relations at McGill University in Montreal, Canada. This led to a 15-year career in marketing, communications, and public relations across a wide range of industries, including oil & gas, automotive, entertainment, beauty and skincare products, and financial services.

Passionate about branding, she is the recipient of three prestigious Advertising Industry Awards for her work on television commercials for the Mercedes-Benz brand in Mexico, including a Cannes Bronze Lion, an Ojo de Iberoamérica, and an A&AD (Global Association for Creative Advertising & Design). She also promotes her passion for branding with talks on luxury brands and marketing at the Universidad Iberoamericana in Mexico City.

While at the BBDO advertising company in Mexico City, Adriana was the leader of the BBDO Inspira program where she delivered workshops for women staff in search of personal and professional balance. In addition, she has been a volunteer and a supporter of programs and organizations of women entrepreneurs to foster gender equality in the professions and workplace.

A deeply committed dog lover for many years, Adriana created Gente Zoo, a foundation in Venezuela for stray animals on the streets, which is supported by a wide range of professionals.

Besides her devotion to her teenage son, her hobbies include traveling, reading, exercising outdoors, and sharing meals with family and friends.

Made in the USA
Las Vegas, NV
21 November 2021